# MANAGING A JUNIOR SOCCER TEAM

# A survival guide for the novice

# MANAGING A JUNIOR SOCCER TEAM

## A SURVIVAL GUIDE FOR THE NOVICE

## Peter Gripton

The Crowood Press

First published in 2001 by
The Crowood Press Ltd
Ramsbury, Marlborough
Wiltshire SN8 2HR

**British Library Cataloguing-in-Publication Data**
A catalogue record for this book is available from the British Library.

ISBN 1 86126 407 0

**Dedication**
To all those parents who stand in the rain and suffer...

Line illustrations by Annette Findlay

Typeset by Phoenix Typesetting, Ilkley, West Yorkshire

Printed and bound in Great Britain by J.W. Arrowsmith, Bristol

# Contents

# Foreword

I have long felt that a book needed publishing for the many hundreds of coaches who look after junior teams throughout the United Kingdom, and that the grass roots of the game is often overlooked when dealing with the development of young players.

Nothing will beat experience but I do believe that the coaching of young players is vital, as it is the first introduction as to whether they will take up the game professionally if they are lucky enough, or will play the game at amateur level, purely for the enjoyment. If bad habits are picked up and not rectified early, it is almost impossible to put players on the right track and too many players' careers have been spoilt by bad practice.

I still believe that the art of coaching is organization, enthusiasm, good information and the coach being unselfish enough to give up his own time in sometimes unsocial hours and poor weather conditions.

The art of coaching is most times in the preparation of the session and the organization beforehand, and failure to prepare can only have disastrous results. My earlier career was spent as a youth coach working in schools and I went on to develop my coaching experience through non-league and professional football, but when in difficulty I always go back to some of my original sessions which include passing and movement in small-sided games.

I believe this book will help coaches at all levels and is uncomplicated but will improve the players' techniques whilst also giving them enjoyment. This will also allow the players to develop as individuals with good technique within the framework of a team game. I have studied football coaching and training techniques in over twenty countries and have coached players who now play at international and Premier League level, and this book will enhance many players' enjoyment in the beautiful game.

Alan Smith
December 2000

# CHAPTER 1

# The Reality of Management

This book is about the *practical management* of junior football teams, based on experience gained over more than seven years of managing nine to twelve-year-olds for both eleven-a-side and small-side football matches. Management in this context means the recruitment, coaching and motivation of a group of youngsters, during the period of some eight months, usually from August through to April, transforming them from new recruits literally 'off the streets', into a cohesive and skilful team.

As a father who was gently pushed into taking over the running of a junior soccer side, I have to admit that I had no credentials for such a task apart from being the only candidate for the job. Like many parents, the involvement came about from my son's interest in football as an eight-year-old. So when it came to writing this book I was acutely aware that I would be laying myself wide open to attack from those who criticize football coaching methods in this country. While the ideal route may be for parents to acquire an FA coaching qualification, in reality most are likely to lack the inclination, time, or most probably, the confidence to undertake such a course of action.

My starting point to becoming a junior soccer coach was by examining the existing literature and videos on the subject. Some were of immense help in providing ideas for training exercises and those which seem to work well for juniors are included here. This reading was supplemented by going on a soccer skills course and observing qualified coaches working at local Centres of Excellence.

On a general level I found many of the books to be pretty humourless and overly complicated. But the lasting impression was that there were a number of basic flaws that ran through all these books, videos and courses.

Firstly, coaching appeared to mean the transferring or teaching of a set of techniques and skills in isolation from the overall objective of producing a football team. These skills were taught to a disciplined and obviously talented group of youngsters who appeared from nowhere, used first-class training facilities and then once they had mastered those skills . . . well, who knows what happened, for then the book, the course or the video finished.

Secondly, many of these books appeared to have been written by people who were, or had been, professional coaches working with very talented and motivated teenagers at the higher levels of the game. But junior footballers are not scaled down sixteen-year-olds. They need to be treated in a different way. They are more fragile than they would admit and a more gentle approach is needed to coax the talent out of a young child, yet this is rarely reflected in the writing.

Even my limited prior involvement with junior football had made me appreciate that there is much more to developing youngsters to play football than purely the application of specific techniques. Ultimately, consistently good football, as in any form of team activity, is about consistently good management. Good management consists of forming and developing relationships with people to help them to achieve common objectives, of getting the best out of the individual to enhance a team situation.

The term 'common objectives' touches upon one of the most important issues in team management. This is reconciling your views as regards the degree and the depth to which competitive attitudes are engendered within the team, with those of the players, parents and the club. Football, by its very nature, is a competitive sport, and you are likely to encounter both managers and parents who encourage highly competitive attitudes, some of which you may find to be a little disturbing and not to your taste. An aspiring manager should have a clear idea of their position on such matters and clearly communicate this to all the parties involved.

Good team management is absolutely vital, yet it is rarely mentioned in coaching manuals. Young players have to contend with poor pitches, well-meaning but sometimes misguided parents, poor refereeing, playing too many matches and poor management. Sometimes it would seem that coaching is the easy part – perhaps that is why there are so many books on the subject.

My experience has taught me that there are a number of common problems that occur with the training of youngsters and producing football teams. When I started I had no guidance on the subject and little assistance and, as a result, no doubt many mistakes were made. This book is therefore an attempt to remedy this situation and hopefully in doing so make some contribution to the improvement of junior soccer.

The main emphasis is on small supervised group activities, the development of ball skills and considerable use of small game play. The number of exercises has been deliberately limited, with greater emphasis on providing advice on how to get players to perform these correctly. These represent the basic skills in which a competent level must be quickly achieved. Bending a ball, diving headers, chips and volleys have been excluded as they are likely to be too advanced for a ten-year-old. There is also no section on tackling; instead, greater emphasis is given to jockeying, pressurizing and covering opponents. For those wishing to go beyond the scope of this book, there are many books readily available which include a far greater repertoire of exercises (*see* page 93).

The objective of this book is that at the end of the first year, your players will have achieved:

- an enjoyment of playing soccer as a leisure activity
- a competence in ball skills
- a basic awareness of tactics
- the ability to work within a team, providing support and marking effectively
- and, hopefully, a few wins along the way.

For the aspiring manager the hope is that this book will whet your appetite to continue improving your knowledge and give you the confidence to obtain an FA coaching qualification.

It has been written in what I hope is a light-hearted manner, not because I don't take the activity seriously, but because there is a need to take a balanced view of what is trying to be achieved. I hope you get as much pleasure out of managing as I have over the years and I wish you the best of luck for the future.

# CHAPTER 2
# A Little Bit About Yourself

Although you are involved in what is supposed to be a voluntary leisure time activity, many managers seem to live in a state of permanent hypertension. So it may be pertinent to stress that there are some desirable personal, as opposed to technical, qualities which are nigh on essential if you are going to achieve some degree of both team success *and* personal satisfaction. Not unreasonably, it is taken for granted that you possess considerable enthusiasm and are fully aware of the considerable commitment in time that will be required.

Firstly, do not underestimate the importance of the task that lies ahead. Coaching young children may not seem to have the glamour of managing a men's team, nor the opportunities to drink considerable volumes of beer, but if you can instil the right attitude into the youngsters, then you will be making a major contribution to their football development. If they are always taught in a methodical and structured manner then this becomes the norm, and as they grow older they will naturally accept this approach and increasingly appreciate its benefits.

Many managers stay with the team as it progresses from perhaps Under 9s through to Under 17s, so there is the opportunity to see the players develop not only as footballers but from youngsters into young men and women. This degree of continuity can be a voyage of discovery for both parties. Not only will they change but so will you, as the relationship changes from one of giving commands to a more mentoring, democratic approach.

Usually the initial worry of a potential manager is to be overly concerned about their own possible lack of footballing skills. It is probably an advantage to have at least played soccer, even if it was only for the primary school second team, but it would seem that most of the best coaches/managers in any kind of sport appear to have been only average competitors themselves. What is much more important is that you can communicate your ideas clearly. If you have limitations, then admit them. Invariably, you will have at least one skilful youngster who you can use to assist you in demonstrating what you require.

You will almost certainly be a parent, you may also manage adults at work, but unless you are a school teacher or involved with cubs or scouts, initially dealing with a group of twenty children can be quite daunting. As an approach, showing tolerance, kindness without it being seen as weakness, and demonstrating a consistent fairness may be a good starting point. You will also need not only an infinite supply of patience and a sense of humour, but the ability to suffer in some degree of silence. This is not easy to achieve, particularly when you may be feeling a little on edge and players are going out of their way to try to wind you up.

You will also need the ability to stand on the touchline in the rain on a cold Sunday morning in January watching your team go down 10–0. It is not a very pleasant experience and it is made worse by a parent bluntly asking what you are going to do about it . . . and you've absolutely no idea. By Sunday afternoon most of the players will have forgotten about the game, but the chances are you won't. All teams get hammered at least once, and some, unfortunately, for most of the time. You really must feel that you can take this kind of result and then have the resilience to pick up the pieces at the next training session and move forward.

Football has been described as a 'magnificent irrelevance'. Well, maybe it is in life's greater scheme, but that is not how little David's father sees it as he storms across the pitch to forcibly articulate his concern as to why his son was not picked for the team. If you are having a bad day then this is the last thing you need. Alas, dealing with parents comes with the territory and is given a chapter of its own because of the situations that can occur.

Remember that it is *their* team, not *your* team. Sometimes managers seem to take a proprietorial stance, giving the impression that the team is obligated to provide entertainment and build the manager's ego. The result is that a poor performance is frequently taken by the manager as a severe personal slight, a situation which is not desirable for either party. Let the team have the glory, while you quietly savour the good moments at a later date.

Lastly, there is a need to keep a sense of perspective. At the end of the day it is just a game. When the team is playing it may be the most important thing in your life, and hopefully theirs as well, but at the end of those sixty or so minutes, whilst it would be nicer to win, a loss should not be seen as one of life's major tragedies. However, no doubt you'll still kick the dog when you get home.

# CHAPTER 3

# Equipment and Facilities

A number of assumptions have been made regarding the type of equipment and facilities required. These are that you are managing the team as part of an existing club set-up, that it has a set of strip, that an acceptable pitch is available and that there is a local league in which the team can participate. This approach has been taken in order to avoid touching upon the sometimes interesting world of football club politics.

As regards competitive leagues for youngsters, my experience has led me to have considerable misgivings as to their value. My belief is that playing friendly matches is ultimately better for developing the skills of young children. In my early days as a manager, the matches were always friendlies with no league tables or points awarded, and in consequence there was far less importance attached to the result, although a win was always nicer than a loss. After Christmas, there would be a Cup competition which everybody took a lot more seriously, but, in general, the nature of all the games provided a better environment in which to learn how to play well. If the opposition arrived with only ten players then we would even lend them a spare player. These arrangements placed less emphasis on putting out the strongest team at every occasion, which has the added disadvantage of leaving many players on the sidelines as permanent substitutes.

Once a league table was introduced, far more gamesmanship emerged, with last-minute cancellations when a team was in danger of being without its star players, and pitch discipline seemed to lessen. Friendlies also allow greater opportunity to rotate the squad so as to ensure that most players have an equal opportunity of playing a match, even though this may mean putting out a weaker team. The largest squads are invariably those with the youngest children, but their numbers usually reduce dramatically as they progress up through the age groups. This means that at the Under 13 level you may only have a squad of eleven players. One of the reasons for this decline in numbers is that at the Under 9 or 10s stage the less able players are rarely given the chance to play on a regular basis. Not unreasonably, they decide to go elsewhere or forget about football. This does nobody any good, as some of those players, whilst slow developers, may have had promising futures.

Squad rotation does tend to develop into a fine balancing act as there will always be a core of competitive players within the team who resent losing when a stronger team was available. Be consoled by the thought that whatever you do, somebody will always be upset.

## EQUIPMENT

### Balls

A size 4 ball is used for up to and including Under 11 teams, both for practice and matches. The ideal is to have one per player; certainly, the absolute minimum requirement should be one ball between two players. For younger players you may wish to try a size 3 ball.

## Cones

Cones are essential, the more the better. The trend is to use multi-coloured sets of small semi-spherical cones or flexible plates, which are relatively cheap and easily transportable. For some activities, road-marking cones are more beneficial, as they make players alter their run pattern, as opposed to running over them. They certainly make better goalposts. Presumably such cones can be purchased, but mine were donated by parents from their places of work, or possibly their local road repairs.

## Bibs

You will need a set of training bibs; these usually come in red, blue, green and yellow.

Good quality ones are not cheap but should be strong enough to survive the considerable amount of wear and tear that they will take throughout the season.

## TRAINING GROUND

For most clubs, training usually takes place outside on the home pitch at the local playing fields, except for bad weather when perhaps use is made of the facilities of a local leisure centre.

It is highly desirable that the pitch should contain a large number of permanently marked adjacent squares, each measuring 10 ˇ 10m. This allows practice sessions which involve exercises in a defined area to be quickly set up, as it minimizes the need to use a large number of cones to define the perimeter. This is a facility which naturally lends itself better to hard, permanent surfaces.

Playing on pitches that are too large is one of the major problems with junior football. Such pitches present a major obstacle to the development of young players and should be avoided wherever possible. Playing on a pitch which is too large places an enormous physical strain on young players, a point not always appreciated by adults. Since 1 September 1998 the maximum size of a pitch for six-a-side teams up to Under 10 has been set at 45m x 36m. No size has been set for the higher age groups.

# CHAPTER 4
# Recruitment of Players

## RECRUITMENT POLICY

It is vital, when recruiting, that you do not undertake auditions to select only the best players. It is utterly absurd to cast aside young players because they do not possess what you consider to be the desired qualities. Children develop at different speeds and there is the risk of eliminating children who with good coaching would probably become excellent players by the ages of twelve or thirteen. All children who wish to train should be given the opportunity to do so. On a more practical note, there will always be a high drop-out rate in the early years. You therefore need as many interested players as possible to ensure that there is a decent-sized squad as it progresses through the age groups.

A suggested recruitment policy would be to approach the head teachers of the local junior schools in July, just before the summer term ends, with details of the training sessions that will commence in August. Depending upon the response, you may need to do a second distribution just after the commencement of the autumn term in September.

Children also operate their own talent-spotting network, where good players from other teams are encouraged, or bribed, to change allegiances, usually on the basis of their performance in the school team.

It is always worthwhile establishing personal contact with your local junior school head teachers. They will invariably know which child exhibits a degree of talent and in consequence can be helpful in getting the child to attend training. It is surprising how many good players at school show a reluctance to attend club training out of shyness or lack of confidence.

There are also an increasing number of head teachers who display a degree of reluctance for children to become involved in competitive games at school, and in consequence show even less enthusiasm to promote the joining of a club, albeit out of school hours. In such cases it is worth stressing in any literature that you hand out, the truism that the games are as much about teaching the children to work together in a co-operative manner as they are about winning. They also help children to appreciate that generally you only get out of life what you put in. It is these kinds of values which are most likely to appeal to such head teachers.

### Player Characteristics

When discussing the personal qualities of younger players, there are a number of issues which are worth exploring.

Many people talk of the need to possess the characteristics of being a team player. Certainly mavericks and hotheads are as likely to lose you a game as win it, but it is often unclear exactly what constitutes the qualities of a team player. Frequently it seems to mean somebody who keeps their head down and doesn't rock the boat. Perhaps it is better for individuals to show both a propensity to think for themselves and signs of self-discipline. Certainly there has to be enthusiasm and this, coupled with an even temperament, is probably more important at such an age than the apparent desire to win. This essentially sums up the right attitude, and with the right attitude you can achieve almost anything.

Secondly, intelligence is an area which, in the formation of a team, should perhaps be valued more highly than it is at present. Intelligence is the only infinite resource that we have and it is suggested that intelligent players are likely to be more articulate, confident and assertive, and quicker to absorb and respond to ideas. To make things worse, they probably already show signs of being smarter than the manager. The highly desirable characteristics of being able to *read the game* and anticipate movement are probably a product of such intelligence. Such players are also more likely to challenge the conventional wisdom of authority. While this may be no bad thing, it is sometimes a characteristic which is not always fully appreciated by managers.

Intelligence is likely to play an important role in determining who will captain the team. Some young children unconsciously display a degree of gravitas which naturally commands the respect of the other team members. They may not be the most skilful players in the team, but they will almost certainly be the most consistent. They will set the standards of play both in training and in the match and will become increasingly important as the team grows older.

The downside is that athletic, academically bright children have such a range of sporting options and choices available to them that football may not hold their interest for more than a couple of seasons. This is particularly true if the team results, or the management, are poor. They are smart enough to know their worth and they will vote with their feet.

In assessing children, most people can easily recognize that the player with pace and dribbling skills has potential and is a joy to watch. But what many may miss is the quiet, less aggressive player who has the ability to make consistently well-weighted passes at the right time and to the right place. This is a valuable skill and in a few years that player's contribution may well be equal to that of the stars up front.

Some very talented players, frequently those who are attackers, can display distinct 'prima donna' attitudes, being very self-centred, with fits of petulance and sulking thrown in for good measure. They can be difficult to manage and coach, as they think they know it all, and some managers see them as a threat to their authority. But these players are matchwinners and if you can live with the frustrations of the downside, they will reward you with some wonderful creative moments. When they are on song they will lift the whole team; when they are down they will take the whole team with them. That is why, for all their talent, they may never achieve the captaincy, for they are rarely capable of feeling and seeing beyond themselves.

However, to a large extent this situation often resolves itself as such players proceed through the age groups. Opposition defences become bigger, faster and smarter while your star player's development stagnates. As a result, they become increasingly less effective and will eventually realize that a different attitude to training and greater integration within the team will benefit everybody, including themselves.

Equally, do not overlook small players – simply because they are small. In the final analysis it is true that a good big 'un will probably beat a good little 'un, but there are far fewer good big 'uns around than people would have us believe.

## Players with Disabilities

If you are contacted by parents whose child has some degree of mental or physical impairment resulting in poor co-ordination, try to be as sympathetic as possible to their request that their child takes part in the training exercises. This is not because they see their child becoming a regular player, but because it gives the child the opportunity to belong, and to be involved in a group activity.

It may be difficult to integrate children with disabilities into some of the group training exercises, but they are likely to gain much pleasure simply from being part of the group, even though their practical involvement may sometimes be minimal. When they take part in a practice game, they will probably rarely touch the ball, but for that short period they will be 'one of the lads'. No training session should ever be so inflexible that it cannot accommodate the needs of such a child.

## Female Players

There has been a huge increase in female soccer teams throughout the world, particularly in the USA. My experience of working with female players has been very limited and has occurred in a mixed team situation. None of the boys ever commented on the fact that there were females in the squad, and I never felt that there was any need to make any special allowances towards them. I treated all the participants simply as equal players and they appeared to respond well.

However, I have been told by managers, invariably male, that junior all-female squads do exhibit some distinct differences from male squads. The females are more polite, they listen better and are more diligent in their approach to training. Sounds like heaven!

## Checklist for the Season

### July
- Begin to have doubts as to why you volunteered to be the manager!
- Approach the headteachers of the local schools and ask if they can distribute leaflets to the appropriate children, publicizing details of the club and the date of the first training session.
- Collect/purchase all the necessary equipment.
- Ensure that the training ground is booked and in good order.

### August
- Use much of the first training session to introduce yourself to the players, the players to each other, obtain all the necessary details on name, age, date of birth, address and telephone numbers, especially mobile phones.

    Consider using the session to play a small-sided game so as to gauge the potential of the squad.

    Set the date of the next session.
- Concentrate on basic skills, passing and small-sided game.
- Send, or better still, hand the parents copies of the club's policies on soccer training. The details of this are explored in the next chapter. Also use this as an opportunity to seek assistants, prepare the parents for the task of joining a kit washing rota and make the first appeal for subscriptions.
- Attend the league meetings for the managers.
- Prepare the match fixture list for the season and give to both the parents and the players.
- Finalize arrangements for regular practice and begin to develop a training plan which outlines the coaching timetable for the season.

### September
- If necessary, undertake second recruitment drive through schools.
- Start chasing those subscriptions.
- Training commences in earnest. Concentrate on basic skills, striking the ball, passing and small-sided game.
- Arrange special sessions for the goalkeeper.

### October
- Concentrate on shooting, dribbling, running with the ball, passing and small-sided game.

### November
- Concentrate on turning, creating space, passing and small-sided game.

### December
- Concentrate on defending, passing and small-sided game.
- Chairman gives you 'his vote of confidence', and so ruins your Xmas.

### January
- The Cup competition commences.
- Concentrate on all aspects of small-sided game.

### February
- Concentrate on creating space, passing and small-sided game.

### March
- Concentrate on all aspects of small-sided game.

### April
- Concentrate on all aspects of small-sided game.

    The season finally ends.

    Organize end of season Dads play Lads match, with the fathers having to wear wellington boots and being limited to playing two-tap football.

# CHAPTER 5

# Dealing with Parents

Whenever a group of junior soccer managers are asked what is the biggest problem they have in organizing their teams, there is always universal agreement that it is the parents who are the major headache. Interestingly, this topic is one that is never addressed in conventional coaching manuals and it makes one wonder just how much practical experience the writers of such books have had with parents.

For many players it will be the first time they have competed in an organized competitive sport outside school. Parents naturally want their child to do well and can be quite vocal in expressing this view. It goes without saying that you need the support of the parents and you will achieve this if you demonstrate that you are both fair and trustworthy. After all, they are placing their children in your care and you are undertaking a considerable responsibility on a voluntary basis. Supportive parents will be able to reinforce the attitudes and techniques you are teaching the boys, and there is probably a strong correlation between a cohesive team and the attitude of their parents.

However, there is a considerable difference between parents being supportive and parents trying to call the shots. Although I have much sympathy for managers who have to endure a difficult relationship with parents, the situation is essentially one of poor management. If you are in charge, then act as if you are in charge, make decisions and

provide clear leadership and direction *from the outset*. Most problems can be resolved by spending some time with the individual parents, but if issues are allowed to fester, eventually they will become unmanageable and have an extremely divisive influence on team performance.

In essence, some kind of contract should be forged with the parents. It is suggested that at the beginning of the season an introductory letter be sent to all parents of new players to ensure that there is a clear understanding of what you are trying to achieve and the requirements placed upon all parties. This letter should form part of standard club policy, but frequently this is not the case and instead each manager is left to his own devices. The letter should contain information on the following:

- the background to the club
- subscriptions, match fees and the strip provided
- the where, when and why of training sessions
- a timetable and dates of league matches and free days
- half-term considerations
- meeting place for away matches
- procedures should a player be unable to attend practice or play in a match
- discipline
- responsibility and behaviour of parents at matches

- policy on the playing of substitutes
- who washes the kit?
- being informed of any illness
- club insurance policy.

Although much of the above information should be straightforward, there are a number of contentious points which parents need to understand clearly and some fairly terse examples of the suggested wording are as follows:

1. Team members are chosen solely on merit, but a large degree of self-selection occurs in as much as those who really want a place make sure they regularly attend practice sessions. A player cannot be selected if he does not come to practice. If your child is a squad member and you are going away for the weekend please try to give as much notice as you can (unfortunately, they rarely do.)

2. It is quite possible that substitutions will be made to try different players in different positions. The policy is that all substitutes will get the opportunity to play during the game. It would be of considerable assistance if you could tell your child that if they are substituted it is not the end of the world. They will always get another opportunity to play a full game.

A small number of friendlies are organized each year and those players who do not command a regular place will have the opportunity to play for the whole game (in these matches).

3. As a parent, please try to attend as many matches as you can. Although they will not

---

**Tips**

The use of substitutes is a very delicate issue. What should be a tactical decision can often become a political decision. Some parents are reluctant to accept that you cannot play with twelve players in order that their child can get a game.

However, managers need to ask themselves why substitutes are being taken along, as it is very unlikely that a child would be injured to the extent that they would have to leave the pitch permanently. The best policy must be to rotate the squad, and either take no substitutes, which does run the risk of a player becoming unavailable on the day of the match, or take a small number who always play. There is little point in taking a weaker player who stands freezing on the touchline and only allowing them to play in the last five minutes of the game. They will only get better by playing, even if doing so temporarily upsets the balance of the team.

---

**Tips**

Junior football often stirs very strong emotional responses in parents. All the more reason, therefore, that you should not allow parents to utter inane, humiliating or abusive comments towards either their own or anybody else's children when they are playing or practising. Remarks such as 'take him out' are totally unacceptable and this stance should never be negotiable.

This kind of comment is unfortunately a both a common and degrading feature of junior football. As soon as such behaviour occurs, stamp it out immediately by having a quick and quiet word with the parent. It may also be as well to examine your actions first, as many parents take the behaviour of the manager as a reference point.

---

dmit to doing so, all the players enjoy the opportunity of demonstrating to their parents how well they can play.

4. All parents are likely at some time to be embarrassed or maybe annoyed by the performance of their child on the pitch. Although it may be difficult, please keep such feelings to yourself and display only positive encouragement. You will find that some of the opposition will have parents who make the most unbelievable comments in the belief that if they verbally abuse their child in public they will play better. All this does is to intimidate, demoralize and confuse the player.

A child is accepted for training on the basis that the parents act in a responsible manner both to the children and other parents. The same applies to responses to the referee's decision; please suffer in silence if you feel a mistake was made.

5. Don't hesitate to ask about your child's progress, but please never insist that they be given a place in the team or play in a particular position.

6. It is greatly appreciated if at the cessation of practice, parents should be there, waiting to take their children straight home.

---

**Tips**

Certainly listen to a parent's concerns but let the team have only one manager – and that's you.

---

# CHAPTER 6

# Assistants

Depending upon the way in which the coaching is structured, you may require the help of some assistants, usually parents of children in the team. Placing a parent in charge of each group where a number of separate training exercises has been set up is of considerable assistance in maintaining discipline. Assistants can also play their part in maintaining some degree of continuity of training should you be late or unavailable.

Sometimes it would seem that it is almost an advantage for a parent *not* to be a skilled player. Any parent with an abundance of natural talent may never have had to spend much time thinking about what to do, and in consequence usually has aspirations beyond what a youngster can deliver at that age and may lack the necessary patience to teach players.

Before training commences in earnest, you may find it worthwhile to bring all the assistants together and explain your plan of action for the season and provide them with both a list of exercises and an explanation of the way in which you intend to implement them.

Your assistants need to understand the general approach that you intend to use and accept that you are in command of the

> **Tips**
>
> Beware of armchair theorists. It can be very irritating to set up a number of different exercises to run concurrently and then see one assistant make modifications to suit their own personal whim or theory.

training. This means that while you will certainly listen to their views, the final decision and responsibility must rest with yourself. Obviously much depends upon your temperament as some people can work well in a committee situation, others less so, but if you do develop a good working relationship progress may well be swifter and more enjoyable than working by yourself.

Many parents will wish to help because their child will be in the squad. They must appreciate that their help does not mean automatic selection of their child for matches. This must also apply to your child. It is desirable that they are regularly substituted so it is seen that they receive no special favours. This is a difficult issue because much of your desire to manage a team comes from seeing your child play, and placing them on the subs bench may understandably dent your enthusiasm.

# CHAPTER 7

# A Training Overview

## TRAINING BASICS

### Realistic Objectives

The most important point to remember is that the training must be enjoyable for both yourself and the players. If it isn't, then why do it?

This isn't to say that it will always be so. Certainly it will be hard work, but at each session there should be the feeling that, with the minimum of aggravation, there has been at least some small degree of improvement.

It is possible that you will enjoy soccer management much more if you realize from the outset that there are considerable limits to what you can achieve in a season. You also need to be realistic about the potential of your squad of players – some years you get dealt a good hand, but in others the deal is not quite so hot. Sometimes you will simply have to take the rough with the smooth.

Assuming that you commence training at weekends in August and finish in early April, then allowing for holidays you will have approximately 50–55 hours of training time and will play approximately twenty-five matches. During this time you will also lose players because of holidays, long weekends, illnesses and visiting Granny. In total, this is not much time with a new group possessing a wide range of abilities. You could, of course, extend the training period or hold mid-week sessions, but this is a commitment that you may be unable to make.

The end result is that there is going to be a considerable amount of training which you will not be able to cover or only barely touch upon. It is desirable then that you set realistic objectives as to the level of attainment to be achieved in the crucial elements of a young player's training.

### Style of Play

From the outset, players need to understand the attitude that you wish to engender, the type and style of play you are trying to achieve and the behaviour which you expect of them both on and off the pitch during the game. As regards the style of play, it is desirable that the players commence their career playing the basics of the kind of football that will be of increasing benefit to them in the higher age groups.

Junior football can be wonderfully entertaining. Apart from whitewash scores such as 18–0, which in truth are games that should be terminated before they get to such a stage, there are games which finish 8–8 or 11–7. These latter games are characterized by fast cavalry charges straight up the pitch against wobbly or non-existent defences whose main task is to boot the ball anywhere so long as it is towards the opponent's half. There would often seem to be a great deal of truth in the saying that English footballers 'run too fast and think too little'.

This type of play is quite understandable at

the Under 10 level, but it is surely inexcusable and unsatisfying at the Under 14 level. The style that is likely to be far more productive would demand that:

• The primary aim of the team should be to play better football, not to win. By consistently playing better football then the wins will occur; simply aiming to win is likely to lead to short-term tactics overriding the development of individual skills.
• The players' primary aim must be to become extremely comfortable on the ball. This means that they can consistently and confidently receive, control and distribute the ball, ideally using either foot.
• The game is slowed down, with well-organized and skilful defences building up attacks from the back.
• The team places an emphasis on maintaining possession of the ball. Players have to be more patient and appreciate that sometimes the ball has to go sideways and backwards as much as it does forwards.
• The players become increasingly proficient in the short passing game, because if they fail to do so, then they will never succeed at longer forms of play.
• Far greater emphasis is placed upon keeping a clean sheet, and once a lead has been built then the emphasis is to maintain this situation and seek further goals 'on the break'.

---

**Tips**

There is a saying that 'motivation gets you going, habit keeps you going'. The players need to develop these necessary skills so that their use becomes an almost automatic response. If they do not develop that level of confidence, then what is the practical use of learning tactics?

---

To play in such a way requires a high degree of skill throughout the entire team combined with good tactical awareness. This is very much a long-term development and common sense should dictate that only limited and patchy progress will be made towards this objective with junior teams.

## Training Session Organization

Before the session begins, ensure that the players have removed rings, watches, necklaces, bracelets and any other items which could cause an injury either to themselves or other players. They should all be wearing shinguards, and you should enquire as to whether anybody is carrying an injury although the chances are that they would never tell you.

Training must never degenerate into a kick around. Every training session should consist of:

• An adequate warm-up.
• A discussion of the last game or session.
• A plan for the day's training, usually built around deficiencies demonstrated in the last match.
• The completion of a set of exercises designed to teach specific techniques or skills to overcome certain faults, the exercises should contain a degree of progression in that once an acceptable level of competence has been achieved a further layer of complexity can be added.
• A small-sided game to complete the session.

This small-sided game is absolutely vital. Even if the rest of the training session has been less than successful, the game must be played for that is what the practice session has been all about.

## Length of Session

Keep the training session to no more than 1½ hours and remember that you will lose some time through latecomers. Arrive early and set up the equipment for the practice sessions so as a prompt start can be made. There can be a temptation with groups of a lower than average standard to increase training time. This would seem to be a logical thing to do, but in practice it only seems to yield rapidly diminishing returns from tired players.

Write down the intended plan of the session's activities, indicating the number of players involved, the size of the area and the approximate time allocated to that activity. It results in a more productive session because there is less likelihood that you will run out of time, or simply forget what you had intended to do.

## Method of Coaching

As regards the style of coaching, initially it would make sense to use the style with which you feel most comfortable. There is no 'best' way of coaching. There are simply some ways which are better than others in certain situations. The skill of course is to know when to use the most appropriate method. As you may

be working with a large group, and hopefully have a clear idea of what you want, then it is suggested that you may find it more productive to use the 'tell–show–tell' principle:

- Tell them why and what they are going to practise.
- Show them the exercise and break down each down into its separate parts.
- Demonstrate with an assistant so as the exercise is undertaken correctly.
- Tell them what they are doing right and wrong as they practise.
- Be prepared to modify the exercise quickly if it is proving to be too difficult for the group. This can be done by simplifying the task, reducing the distances involved, increasing the time limits, allowing more touches of the ball or reducing its speed and height.

As the players progress then it may be more beneficial to work in smaller groups and possibly on an individual basis. This of particular relevance for the less skilled players. In these circumstances, a softer approach which involves getting players to analyse and suggest ways of overcoming their limitations, or particular situations, may be more productive. Players need to appreciate that 'practice makes permanent'. Unfortunately, this applies to both good and bad habits, so bad play needs to be eradicated as quickly as possible.

They also need to train as they intend to play. This is largely more a question of attitude than physical effort. Certainly if concentration and the degree of application is poor at practice, there is good chance that the team is beaten before they play the match.

Try to be as positive as possible at all times, and praise as often as you can without devaluing the standards you are expecting the players to achieve. Don't engage in sarcasm, ridicule or indulge in mindless shouting. If you get exasperated keep it to yourself and attempt to ease the situation with a little light humour.

When coaching, always concentrate on improving one aspect of play at a time. It is very easy to try to cover a number of aspects at one time with the result that little improvement is made in any of them.

## Bad Behaviour

The majority of your players are likely to be boys, and they will usually display a healthy exuberance of spirit. Sometimes this exuberance degenerates into rudeness and you should take the time to explain to them what you consider to be both acceptable and unacceptable behaviour.

Bad behaviour in my experience is very rare, but if it occurs be firm and nip it in the bud immediately. The approach should be to explain why the child's specific bad behaviour is unacceptable, rather than describing the child in general terms as being unacceptable. If the behaviour persists discuss the problem with both the parent *and* the child at the end of the session. This invariably solves the problem.

If persistent bad behaviour extends simultaneously to a number of players then it may be advisable if you examine your style and methods, as the fault may lie with yourself.

It is generally preferable for parents not to attend training sessions as spectators as they can be a distraction, or, more unfortunately for them, be considered as an ever present source of embarrassment by their offspring.

## Less Intensity for the Very Young

When dealing with groups of very young players, perhaps aged seven or eight, the aim should be to:

- use a size 3 ball
- reduce the overall level of intensity of the training session
- train for no longer than an hour
- keep to the easier exercises
- keep the buzz going with plenty of variety in the exercises
- allow more rest time
- play more small-sided games, with less interruption to remedy mistakes.

Chapter 11, on small-sided games, spends more time on the different coaching approaches required when dealing with different age groups.

You will no doubt become aware that the attitude of young players can appear to be very selfish, as it would seem to revolve solely around themselves and the ball. It is a phase they go through, and they will grow out of it, although sometimes you doubt whether it will be in your lifetime.

## Keeping the Buzz Going

Depending upon the number of players and assistants available, it is usually advantageous to attempt to divide them into three or four smaller groups, each of which practises a different exercise for 15–20 minutes before rotating. Wherever possible, structure the exercises so that as many players as possible are actively engaged in the activity. This not

---

**Tips**

If things are not going well, calm down and be prepared to 'go with the flow'. Ask the players what they would like to do – invariably it will be to play a game – and go along with their wishes.

---

only avoids boredom setting in but just as importantly keeps the players warm on a cold day.

Young players have short attention spans and consequently will frequently complain that an exercise is 'boring'. Although it is easy to bemoan their apparent attitude, much of this originates from the coach. Not only is there a need to keep a 'buzz' going during the exercises, but the players need to be progressively pushed onto more complex tasks where at each stage the definition of what is the minimum standard required is made quite clear to them.

## Homework

As your practice time with the players may be limited then perhaps you should consider giving them homework. They should be shown what to practise and told they will be examined in that particular routine at the next session.

## At the End of the Session

Although most parents will have arrived before the session finishes to collect their children, there will always be occasions when they are late. Fortunately, this does not usually occur very often, and while it can be annoying, you should not allow a child to be left waiting alone in what may be a relatively secluded public area. I would strongly suggest that you adopt the policy of not leaving the training field until the matter is resolved. Attempt to 'phone the parents to see what the problem is, and if this is unsuccessful, then drive or escort the child back home.

## WARMING UP

Whilst nobody would doubt the benefits of systematic warm-up sessions, in practice youngsters rarely undertake them properly and so their value is likely to be greatly diminished. Young footballers usually see training solely in terms of using a football, at this age level they are much more likely to respond well to a warm-up which commences with light exercises using a ball. The fact the ball is being used has much more meaning for the players. It is said that it is difficult to get Brazilian players to practise without the ball, and what's good for them may well be good for your squad.

What is important is that the players appreciate that some form of warm-up is necessary at the beginning of every training session. In that way, the transition to more extensive and conventional warm-up exercises can be painlessly achieved in later years.

One way to introduce such an idea is to tell players that when they arrive for the training session, they should get into the habit of taking a ball and commence exercises either singly or in pairs with the minimum of direction from the manager. This develops self-discipline and makes for more productive use of the limited time available.

A typical warm-up session could be along the following lines:

• Each player has a ball and dribbles within a defined area, changing direction using a variety of turns, at the blow of the whistle.

Vary the speed of the exercise as well as which foot they should use and which direction they should turn. It is also useful if you dictate the type of turn and the direction by using your hands rather than your voice. This encourages the players to keep their heads up when on the move.

• One player dribbles the ball while another player attempts to get it from him without actually tackling. The player with the ball should use one foot to control the ball and swap to the other at the blow of the whistle. This encourages shielding, turning and dribbling skills.

• Divide the players into pairs and let them lightly jog within a defined area, passing the ball between them.

# CHAPTER 8

# Basic Skills

These are all perfectly straightforward exercises which are broken down into a number of distinct areas, each with a different objective. The players have got to be able to achieve a high level of proficiency in these basic skills, so that their response to a given situation becomes almost automatic.

The usual way to commence such training is for a series of squares to be marked out so that pairs of players can work with each other in carrying out the exercise. The only problem with this approach for young players is that they need a consistently well delivered ball, which may be beyond the capabilities of their young colleague.

For that reason it is suggested that initially groups of up to five players are arranged to stand in a 120-degree arc, some five paces from the coach. One assistant works with you so that you can demonstrate each exercise, then you deliver the ball to each player in turn so that they receive individual attention. This is a slow process, which is not particularly desirable on a cold day as it leaves so many players standing waiting, but it does deliver the results and once a good level of competency has been achieved the children can then be arranged into pairs. One problem that you will immediately face is that the players will remain stationary and expect the ball to come exactly to them. Wait until they have achieved a degree of proficiency, and then you can then begin to vary the pace and direction of the ball. Once all the exercises have been completed throw or kick the ball at random, telling them the kind of response you want.

This is also the appropriate time to explain the phrase 'keeping your eye on the ball'.

*Training semi-circle.*

Soccer is a game requiring a very high degree of mainly foot/eye co-ordination. From the players' own experiences of football, tennis, squash and cricket, they should be able to relate to the habit of closing their eyes, or diverting their gaze towards the area where they wish the ball to land, *a fraction of a second before contact is made.* The result is usually a miss or poor ball contact. The players need to appreciate the need to make a conscious effort to maintain eye contact with the ball especially when passing or shooting and they should soon find a definite improvement in their accuracy.

## BALL CONTROL SKILLS

The objective is that the player becomes increasingly confident in their ability to stop and control the ball as it approaches from a variety of heights, angles and speed.

For the heading exercise set up two parallel lines of cones 5m wide and 5m apart, with a player between each cone facing a colleague. For the other exercises, extend the distance between the two parallel lines to 10m.

With younger players, some managers find it preferable to use a light plastic ball initially for the heading exercises.

As the players become more proficient in the various exercises, you can increase both the width and distance between the cones, vary the speed, angle and trajectory of the ball, and vary the degree of bounce, if applicable.

## Heading

For this exercise:

- Move quickly to a position behind the line of the ball.
- Stand with one leg behind the body so as to make the stance more secure.
- Bend backwards and tilt the head back so as to use the neck muscles to give further leverage.
- Keep an eye on the ball at all times.
- Move the upper body and head forward and make contact with the middle of the ball on the forehead, not the top of the head.

The ball should accelerate away from the forehead faster than when it hit, and should go straight back into the hands of the thrower.

*Ball control training squares.*

## Attacking Headers

In this exercise, each player acts alternately as goalkeeper and thrower of the ball. The receiver of the ball attempts to head the ball between the opposing cones by beating the goalkeeper. The best way to achieve this is to head the ball into the low corners. To do this, the forehead will need to make contact with the upper part of the ball to ensure it moves downwards.

## Defending Headers

The set-up is the same as attacking headers, except that the forehead hits the lower half of the ball. The objective is to achieve distance by placing the ball over the head of the thrower.

## Chesting the Ball

Considerable emphasis should be placed on the ability to chest a ball because there are

*Moving the body back to take the pace out of the ball.*

many instances where to do so is likely to yield far greater benefits than heading the ball. While many players are prepared to head the ball, in a match situation it is rarely directed into an advantageous position and an opportunity is wasted.

For this exercise:

- Stand as for heading, keeping arms away from the body to ensure that the ball does not hit them (which could be judged to be handball). Move into the line of the ball, ensuring that the body is kept square at all times to the direction of the ball.
- Demonstrate how the ball bounces straight off the chest if the chest remains stationary.
- Now as the ball approaches move the chest back so as to take the pace out of the ball. Keep an eye on the ball at all times.
- Take a small step back for the ball to fall to the feet. Trap with the foot. With sidefoot push the ball forward and then again with sidefoot push the ball back to the thrower.

## Controlling with the Feet

Use the sidefoot to demonstrate how the ball bounces straight back off if the ankle remains 'locked'.

Move into the line of the ball. As the ball approaches keep an eye on the ball and 'soften' the ankle so as to take the pace out of the ball. The sidefoot is used because it has a greater area for the ball to come into contact with and in consequence is easier to control. Make sure that the foot is raised so that it touches the centre of the ball. If the foot remains on the ground then there is a risk it will bounce up over the foot and make a return pass more difficult.

When the ball comes to rest it should be resting against the sidefoot as though it was stuck with glue. The natural inclination of young players is to take a step back so that they

29

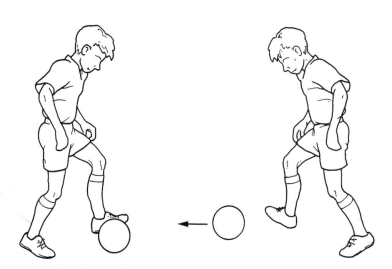

*Trapping the ball with the side foot.*

can then strike the ball. What they should in fact do is tap it forward and then strike it. However, the ideal situation is to judge the 'softness' of the ankle so that the ball bounces one or two feet forward off the foot to eliminate the need for this extra tap.

Practise this exercise with either foot, then progress the practice so that the children control with one sidefoot and pass back with the other. Finally, progress the practice so that they control with the outside of the foot and return with the sidefoot. This should be done as one continuous movement. Practise with either foot.

## Controlling a Bouncing Ball with Sidefoot

The previous exercise will have been carried out with the ball rolling over the surface, but the children are just as likely to have to face a bouncing ball.

In this exercise, practise as before, but throw the ball so that it bounces a few feet in front of the player. The player will need to raise their sidefoot to reach the ball.

*When passing with the sidefoot, strike the centre of the ball so it travels flat across the pitch.*

This is a difficult exercise for youngsters to master because they often take their eye off the ball. Consequently they completely misjudge the bounce and the ball passes under their foot or over their leg. This can be disastrous for defenders, so if progress in this skill is slow they should remember that as a safe alternative that they should get their body behind the ball. Practise the exercise with either foot.

## Controlling the Ball with the Thigh

If you have a good group who have progressed well, try this exercise – it's not easy.

The upper thigh has to be raised *before the ball hits the leg* and then lowered to take the pace out of the ball exactly as if it were the side-foot. Most players raise their leg too late, with the result that the ball hurtles off into space. Practise this exercise with either thigh.

*Bringing the thigh down to cushion the ball.*

## Striking the Ball

The objective is that the player can strike the ball with specific areas of the feet to achieve the required degree of speed, height and accuracy. Those areas are:

- The **inside toe,** which is defined as the area above and to the rear of the big toe. This achieves medium power and distance through the air.
- The **drive,** which is through the laces. This achieves maximum power and distance horizontal to the ground.

There are two things that players should remember at all times when hitting the ball:

- Always go for accuracy first, the distance will come later when you have the confidence to use full power.
- Keep your eye on the ball at all times.

## Using the Inside Toe

This generates what is known as a lofted pass, the ball attaining a height of approximately twice that of the players' height. In this exercise:

- Practise in pairs in a 10 x 30m box.
- The non-striking foot should be pointed at the target and alongside, but not too close to the ball.
- Use a curved run-up approach and make contact with the ball on its lower right or left of centre.
- Do not lean back or the toe will not be properly placed under the ball.
- Follow through with the striking leg.
- An allowance will need to be made for the wind strength and direction once the ball has left the ground as well as the slight spin given through hitting it off centre.

*The inside toe is the shaded area.*

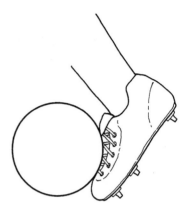

*Driving the centre of the ball with the laces.*

## Driving the Ball

This generates a shot of considerable power in a straight line which travels both low and parallel to the ground:

- Practise in pairs in a 10 x 30m box.
- The chest must be square to the target as that decides the direction of the ball.
- Keep eye on the ball – do not look up at target, however tempting it may be.
- Take a relatively straight run-up approach to the ball.
- Place the non-striking foot by the side of the ball.
- The head must be over the ball; do not lean back or the ball will go into the air.
- Keep the toes of the striking foot pointed down.
- Hit the ball on its centre with the laces. Allow the leg to follow through with such a force that both feet may leave the ground.

## Moving Ball Situations

The previous exercises have used a dead ball situation, but this only occurs in a minority of situations in an actual game. The player therefore need to practise striking moving balls towards a defined target, with the ball being delivered to them at a variety of angle and pace.

Keeping an eye on the ball is absolutely vital, as is the need to allow for differences in the placement of the non-striking foot. A ball coming from behind will need the foot placed in front of the ball and vice versa for a ball from directly ahead. Balls coming in at right angles run a considerable risk of being hooked or sliced. It may be better in these circumstances if younger players attempt to control the ball with the first touch before striking it.

### Tips

This is an exercise which you'll soon know if you're doing well. If you hit the ball too high above the centre, it will feel as if your ankle is coming apart; if you hit it too low then you stub your toe on the ground.

# SHOOTING

## Shooting from Angles

Ideally, this should be undertaken in the penalty area using a full size goal. It requires three players, one goalkeeper and one ball retriever.

The three players are spread out on the edge of the penalty area facing the goal with the outermost player at the corner of the box. The middle player passes the ball forward to the outermost player who pushes it forward and then shoots at the goal. The essential points are:

- There must be a good first touch from the striker of the ball.
- The shot should be low, hard and across the goal to the far post.
- The other two attackers should run straight towards the goal so that they can strike any balls which the goalkeeper either misses or deflects.
- Practice should be carried out from both sides of the penalty area using either feet.

## Overhead Delivery

The set-up is the same as in 'shooting from angles', but this time the ball is lobbed by the coach gently over the head of the outermost player who cannot move until the ball is seen.

## Rear Delivery

The set-up is the same, but this time the ball is delivered by the coach from both alongside and behind the player.

## Front Delivery

The set-up is the same, but this time the ball is delivered towards the player from the goal line.

## Quick Shooting

This uses either the penalty area or a similar sized area with full width goals. This exercise requires six players, one goalkeeper and one ball retriever.

One player is positioned on the outer edge of each of the three sides of the penalty area

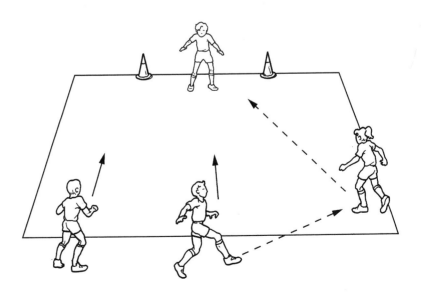

*Shooting exercise.*

33

with a supply of balls and given the number one, two or three. The remaining three players remain within the area. When the number one, two or three is called the appropriate player passes a ball into the area.

Initially, divide the three players into two attackers and a defender. As the ball is played into the area the attackers attempt to gain possession of the ball and shoot at the goal as soon as possible. The first attacker to the ball has the option of being allowed one pass and the receiver of the ball has two touches to control and shoot. No cheating is allowed! The players need to be aggressive, controlling the ball and shooting as soon as they can. The defender's task is to place the ball outside the area.

As their competency increases, remove the defender so that it is one on one, and then make it three players competing against each other.

## PASSING

### Passing Skills 1

Set up as illustrated with players *standing inside* the cones which are set 10 to 15m apart:

- Initially the players pass the ball clockwise and anti-clockwise, and then in a figure of eight arrangement.
- Make sure that the body is kept open by not being square to the ball; this allows easier onward movement of the ball.
- Do not sacrifice accuracy for speed and keep the head up.
- Initially the players should play two-tap but this can be reduced to one-tap as they progress.
- Use permutations of one and two feet using the inside and outside of the foot.

*Quick shooting exercise.*

*Passing skills 1.*

To extend the exercise, give each player a number; the player receiving the ball has to pass to the player whose number has been selected at random by the coach. Keep this continuous. The emphasis is on the quality of the first touch.

## Passing Skills 2

Set up the exercise initially for continuous two touch passing, then move to continuous one touch passing. Progressively shorten both the distance between the two groups and the width of the centre cones as play improves.

Make sure the ball is struck so that it keeps on the ground.

### Spinning Off

With older players this exercise can be altered to practise 'spinning off' a defender. This is a technique by which players can lose a defender when playing with their backs towards the opposition's goal

In this exercise, the player about to receive the ball needs his colleague next in the queue to close up and act as a defender whose intention is to prevent him turning. Rather than do

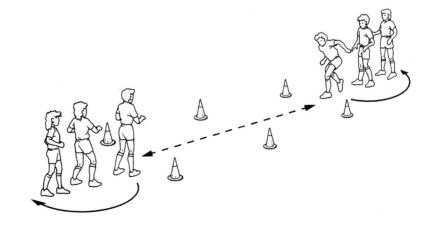

*Passing and spinning off.*

*Standing side-on to the defender allows the attacker to see both them and the ball.*

*Playing side-on allows the player greater ease to spin off and evade the defender.*

so, the player passes the ball back and then turns very tightly, or spins, to face the opposite direction and run behind and beyond the defender.

### Playing 'Side On'

This exercise is even more effective if the player about to receive the ball turns sideways to the ball so that they can see both the passer of the ball and, out of the corner of their eye, the defender. This allows them greater awareness of the defender's response and eases their ability to move clear. Ensure that the players practise on both sides so that they can return the ball with either foot.

### Follow the Ball

This is a continuous exercise which should be undertaken at a slow initial pace and then speeded up. It commences as two-tap and then moves to one-tap:

- player A passes to player B
- player A then follows ball to end of player B's queue
- player B passes to player C and follows the ball to the end of player C's queue and the cycle continues
- change direction and use different permutations of the feet.

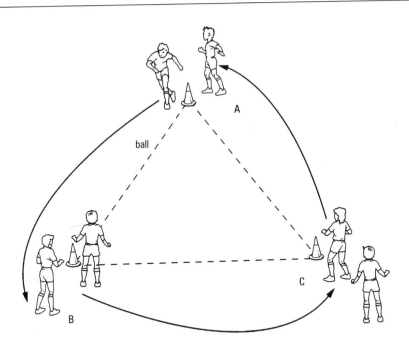

ball

A

B

C

*Follow the ball.*

## Give and Go

Set up the cones to define an area of 50 x 10m and undertake a demonstration with an assistant. The secret to doing this correctly is to:

- Run at a slow pace and only speed up when the passing becomes consistently accurate
- Have the assistant act as player A until a

reasonable degree of proficiency has been achieved.

- Have the players run *in a straight line* between the two cones, receiving, controlling and then passing the ball.

To commence the exercise, player A has the ball and passes it both diagonally and ahead of player B so that it arrives just ahead of his feet

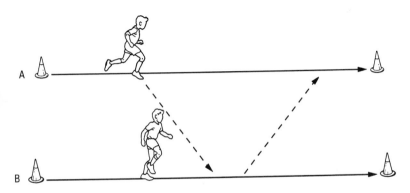

A

B

*Give and go.*

## Tips

The sequence of events should be that the space is created, the ball is delivered and the player arrives. Invariably the latter two are reversed and the player's tempo is affected as they have to wait for the ball.

as he runs in a straight line towards the cone. The quality of B's first touch, pushing the ball forward, is very important. Once player A has passed the ball he accelerates forward ahead of his teammate so as to receive the return pass, and so the cycle continues.

Start off with three-tap possession and reduce to two and then one-tap as the players become more proficient. Once the cones are reached they can either reverse the procedure and come back to the start or simply sprint back and leave the area free for the next pair.

Once the players have become proficient with this exercise, another player, in the role of a defender, should be directed to advance down one line of play. As the pair advance, the player with the ball passes to his colleague and then runs forward, both past and behind the defender, before receiving the ball back.

## Four-Corner Passing

This is a continuous exercise which should initially be undertaken at a slow pace and then speeded up.

Set up a 20–25m square box with at least two players at each corner. Initially use one ball.

Player A passes the ball to B, and then runs towards B. Player B passes the ball back to A, and then runs off towards C. As soon as A receives the ball back they pass it directly to C and continue forward to take B's place. As soon as C receives the ball they pass it to D who returns it to C and then runs towards A and so the cycle continues. Both the ball, and eventually all the players, will circulate around the cones. Alter the rotation so that the players have to use their non-striking foot.

Once this is working well, then two balls can be used simultaneously, with play commencing at diagonally opposite cones. Using two balls makes the task considerably more difficult.

Once this has been achieved, the session can be upgraded. Go back to using one ball and modify the procedure so that when A receives the ball back from B he passes it directly back

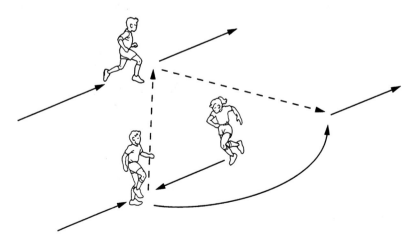

*Give and go with defender.*

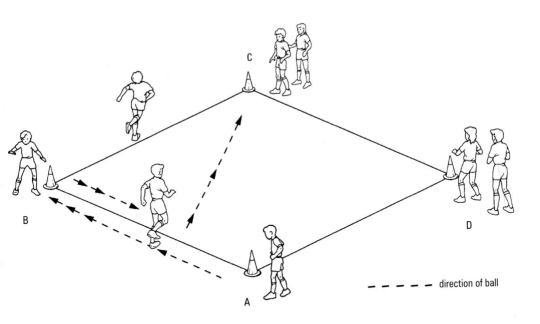

*Four-corner passing.*

to B who is running towards C. This needs an accurately weighted pass so as B is able to pass the ball to C, ideally with one touch. As soon as C receives the ball he passes it to D and so the new cycle continues.

Once players have mastered this new aspect of the exercise two balls can again be used simultaneously, with play commencing at diagonally opposite cones.

## Take and Drag

As youngsters have a habit of running into each other, this is an exercise that achieves something productive when they do so:

- Set up a 20 x 20m square with players at each corner. Initially two sessions operate in parallel.
- Players A and B run towards each other. Player A has the ball and as they converge,

B, *the player without the ball,* calls out 'take' or 'drag'.

- 'Take' tells A that the ball is to be left alone and B will take control of it in *front* of the player and pass it to A's cone.
- 'Drag' means that the ball is to be reversed in the opposite direction by the sole of A's

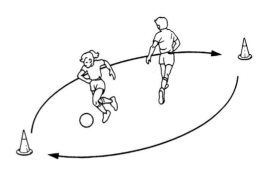

*Take and drag.*

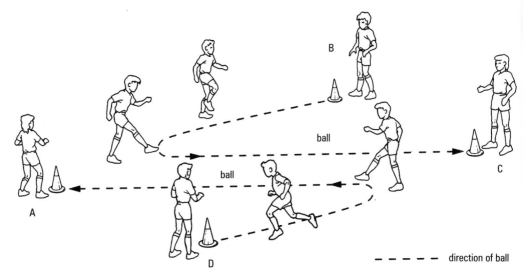

*Take and drag with passing movement.*

- - - - - - direction of ball

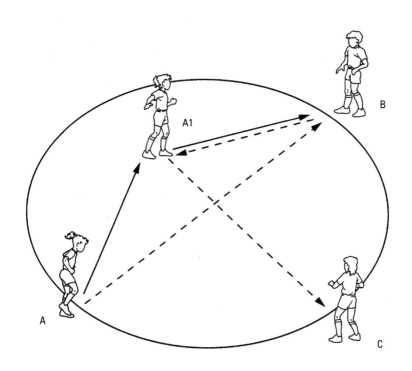

*Passing across the circle.*

foot and B will take control of it *behind* A and pass it to A's cone.

Once this is working well, then a passing movement is added.

Commence play with a ball at opposite corners A and C. As soon as the player from B receives the ball, they have to turn and pass it back to cone C. Likewise, the player from D has to pass it back to A. This will make them use their right foot to pass.

Then commence play from corners B and D; this will use the players' left feet.

## Passing Across the Circle

Arrange the players to stand on the edge of a circle 20–25m in diameter.

Player A passes the ball to B, and then follows the ball into the circle. B returns the ball to A, and follows the ball into the circle. A passes it to C. A then finishes their run by taking B's place on the edge of the circle. C passes the ball to B, who then passes it to D. B finishes their run in A's place. D passes the ball to C, and so the cycle continues.

This should commence as a two-tap exercise and move to one-tap. Ensure that both feet are used.

## Figure of Eight Passing

Players A and B each stand at cones which, depending upon the age group, are spaced between 15–25m. To commence, player C stands alongside B and passes to A. They then follow the ball, running tightly around and behind A, who pushes the ball forward so that C can now pass it to B, and so the cycle continues. Each player should make a number of continuous circuits.

If done correctly, this is a very useful, high-intensity exercise, but it does have a number of possible pitfalls:

- The players must take a figure of eight course, not a circular course, so that both feet are used alternately for the passes.
- Players A and B must be alive and alert, as their ability to control the ball and lay off a well-weighted pass is of equal importance.
- The players should run at the same pace throughout the exercise, maintaining fast leg movement by taking smaller steps as they run around A and B.

## Overlaps

- Players A and B are 10m apart as they begin to run forward towards C. B passes to C,

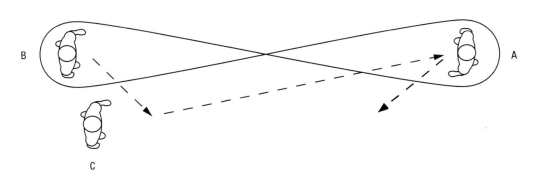

*Figure of eight passing.*

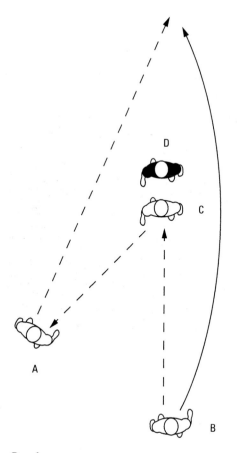

*Overlaps.*

*The ball must be behind the head, and the front foot on but not over the line.*

and then sprints forward into the vacant space behind defender D.

- C lays off the ball to A, who makes a well-weighted pass so that it is received by B as he is on the move.
- The ball should arrive first, followed by B, and not the other way around.
- The exercise can be completed by B taking a shot at a goal.

## Throw-In Skills

The throw-in should be regarded simply as a different kind of pass whereby the thrower is not pressured by the opposition. The laws of soccer say that the ball must be held clearly behind the head in both hands, and at the time of releasing the ball, both feet must be on the ground, either on or behind the line.

And that is exactly what must be practised. There can be a run-up to the line or the player can throw the ball from a stationary position. To perform a throw-in, arch the body back and bend the knees to get extra leverage, making sure that the ball is clearly behind the head.

Demonstrate what you require and then using groups of players, have them take turns in making throw-ins to you from a line on the ground so as to make the exercise as realistic as possible.

Next, break the group down into pairs. They alternately throw the ball to each other,

*This is poor marking. The defender is ball-watching and allowing the opponent to go behind him with a straight run to the goal.*

*Now the defender is goalside of the opponent and can see both him and the ball.*

taking it on the chest, or at the feet, and returning it. Once progress is being made in this area, attention can now be given to improving throw-ins and associated marking skills.

Working with an assistant and using a player as opposition, you can emphasise the need to mark the player by standing behind them, on a line drawn *between* the player and a designated goal. This allows you to watch *both* the player and the ball.

You should demonstrate the dangers of:

- standing in front of the opponent;
- standing too close to the player, for there is every likelihood that the ball will be thrown over your head and the player will *spin off* and disappear behind you.

Demonstrate the need to keep a distance and only move towards the player as the ball is thrown, finally, emphasise that throw-ins should be taken as quickly as possible to secure the best advantage.

*The correct position for throwing-in.*

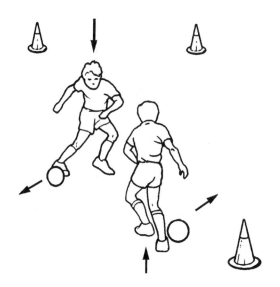

## DRIBBLING

The objective is for the player to keep the ball under close control when moving forward and avoid dispossession. This exercise requires a 10 x 10m square.

As the attacker approaches the defender they drop a shoulder, in the diagram it is on their left, giving the impression that they are intending to move in that direction, then at the last moment they move the ball with the outside of the foot to the right and pass the opponent on that side. The move to the right needs to be quick and positive, with acceleration away from the defender.

Young players often find this difficult to co-ordinate, usually preferring to use pace to pass a defender. To overcome this, the players should face and then run at each other, dropping the *same* shoulder and accelerating away in the opposite direction. Failure to drop the same shoulder will result in a major pile-up! It may help if players initially undertake this exercise without using a ball.

*The attacker drops their left shoulder and feigns a move to the left.*

44

*The defender takes the bait and the attacker now pushes the ball with the outside of their right foot in the opposite direction.*

*The attacker now moves to the right, past the defender who is off-balance and cannot respond.*

---

### Tips

Coaches sometimes give the impression that anything can be coached, but the ability to dribble well seems to depend very much on an abundance of natural talent. You either have it or you don't. Young players can often seem to dribble well, but they are frequently aided in this by the poor defending techniques of the opposition. If a player is having some success with dribbling then it would be foolish to attempt to change his style. However, it should be pointed out that dribbling can be both a slow and sometimes risky way of gaining territorial advantage. Virtuoso displays which result in regular dispossession are of no value.

If the player is not confident in dribbling, nor has clear-cut pace to pass an opponent, then they should adopt the habit of passing the ball before a possible tackle takes place, and then move into the space.

## RUNNING WITH THE BALL

Running with the ball means precisely that – run with the ball. It is not meant to be a gentle stroll down the touchline with the eyes glued to the ball.

For this exercise, set up an angled 40 x 20m box. The player at cone A receives, controls and pushes the ball forward with the side-foot. They then keep the ball ahead of them by using the laces, providing sufficient power so as a full strided run can be maintained. At cone B the ball is passed to the waiting player at cone C and the cycle is continued.

To assist in maintaining a regular rhythm, the players should count out the number of strides they take, usually four or five, before they touch the ball forward again. It is also essential that each player keeps their head up while running, otherwise it defeats one of the prime objectives of the exercise.

At a later stage, once they touch the ball for the second time, have them pursued by the person next in line.

## TURNING SKILLS

The objective is that the player is able to move confidently away from an opponent to achieve a more advantageous position whenever the situation presents itself. Turning should be considered as an essential ingredient of creating space.

### Inside and Outside Hook

This exercise should be carried out by the trainer and an assistant, initially at walking pace. Some trainers advocate stopping the ball with the sole of the foot, but youngsters seem to find this difficult at higher speed

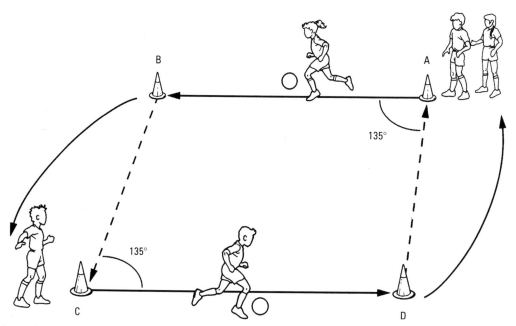

*Running with the ball.*

*The non-striking leg needs to bend to allow the player to decelerate and have a stable body position.*

*The outside of the right foot pushes the ball back and quickly clear of the feet.*

so the use of a hooked foot is to be preferred.

The player moves off dribbling the ball and is shadowed by the opponent who makes no attempt to dispossess him. The position of the ball relative to the feet will determine the type of turn to be made. For an inside turn with the right foot, the ball needs to be on the left; for an outside turn with the right foot, the ball needs to be on the right.

When the player wishes to turn they move their non-striking leg forward of the ball and allow it to bend and take all the weight of de-acceleration. It is vital to bend the leg so as to aid control of the ball and provide a platform to reaccelerate. As the player does this, they turn their back towards the opponent so that their body is always between the opponent and the ball. If they turn to face the opponent, which so many of them initially do, then the opponent has an easy opportunity to dispossess them.

As the player comes to a momentary stop the striking foot moves forward of the ball and stops its movement by trapping it with the inside or outside of the foot and then sweeps it back in the reverse direction.

It is imperative that the ball must be swept forward quickly to clear the feet. The player then follows the ball and dribbles it back to the starting point. Allow the player to dribble the ball some 10m before turning. Ensure that they practise using both feet.

*Inside and outside hook.*

## Cruyff Turn

Apart from being very effective, this kind of turn appeals to those youngsters who enjoy being a little 'flash'. Unlike the other two types of turn, the player now faces the opponent.

As before, the position of the ball relative to the feet will determine the type of turn to be made. To use the right foot, the ball needs to be on the right:

- When the player wishes to turn, they move their non-striking leg forward of the ball and pivot towards the opponent. Failure to pivot will cause the ball to hit, or be trapped between the legs.
- As the player comes to a stop, the inside of the striking foot traps the ball and pushes it behind the other leg. The ball is now moving in the reverse direction.
- The ball must be pushed back quickly to

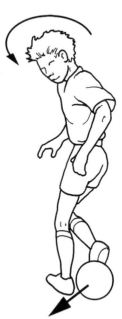

*Cruyff turn.*

Inside hook using right foot

Outside hook using right foot

Cruyff turn using right foot

*Direction of turn using right foot.*

clear the feet. The player then continues pivoting, follows the ball and dribbles it back to the starting point. Allow the player to dribble the ball some 10m before they turn. Ensure that they practise using both feet.

## Turn and Pass

This exercise is exactly as above, but once the ball has changed direction it is passed back to a stationary supporting colleague. Once this is working well, the player with the ball can be allowed to make longer runs. Once a gap of 10–15m has opened up between them and their supporting colleague, the colleague then commences to follow him so as to make the exercise more realistic.

## Turn, Pass and Receive Back

The previous exercise should progress so that once the ball has been passed back, the player runs *behind* the defender and into space so as to receive the ball back from their supporting colleague. This exercise can be extended so that once the supporting player has passed the ball, they then run forward past the defender to receive the ball back.

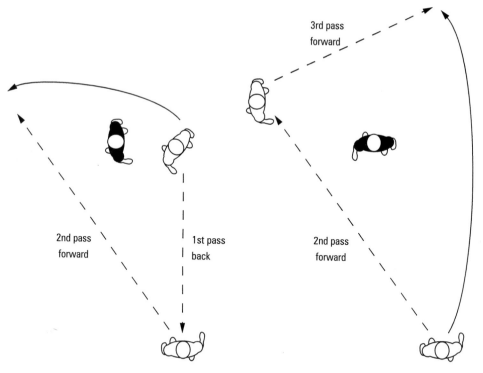

3rd pass
forward

2nd pass
forward

1st pass
back

2nd pass
forward

*Turning, passing and receiving back.*

## CREATING SPACE

Up to now the players have been engaged in largely repetitive exercises. Now they have to use greater initiative and begin to learn to move into space. By moving into space, players are placing themselves in a position which allows them greater opportunity to receive the ball. Ideally, the space into which the player moves should allow the ball to move towards the opposition's goal.

### Movement around the Box

For this exercise, you will need an area of 10–15m square. You will need a minimum of five players.

Initially, one player is allocated to the outside of each of the four sides, while one player remains in the centre. The objective is for the outer players to pass the ball to each other without it being intercepted by the player in the middle. To do so they will need to keep moving along their allocated touchline so as to place themselves into the most advantageous position for passing and receiving. Proceed for periods of one minute and then change the person in the centre.

As the players become more proficient so they should be restricted to using only half the length of each side.

The square can be reduced in size, or increased with two players allocated to each side. When using two players to a side, they cannot pass the ball to their colleague – it must be to a player on one of the other three sides.

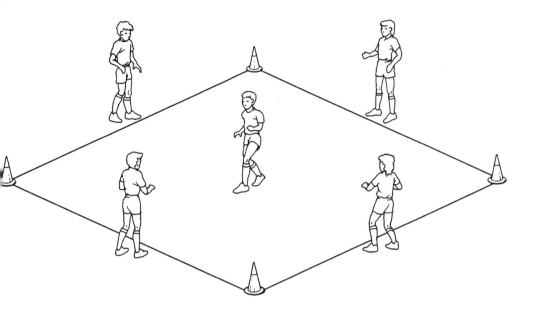

*Full movement around the box.*

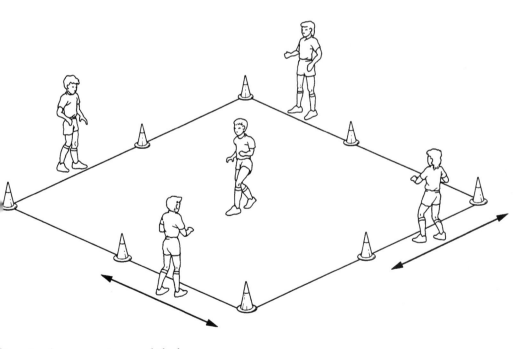

*Restricted movement around the box.*

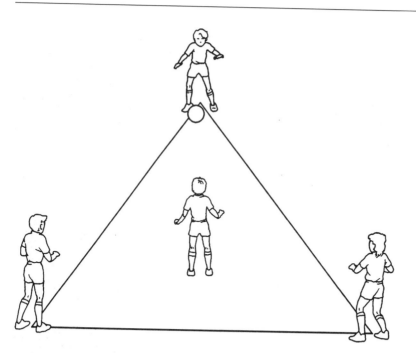

*Triangular support play.*

## Piggy in the Middle

Now that the players have demonstrated an ability outside the square, it is time for them to work together inside the area. The ability to

do this exercise well is a key indicator as to whether you have the makings of a good team, and the players should be left in no doubt as to the importance that they should attach to this exercise.

You will need an area of 15x15m which is well defined, preferably by tape, although you can use cones. Commence with 4 v 1, where the single player is the defender, or piggy, who has to intercept a pass between the other four players, all of whom must work within the square. The four players have to maintain possession by passing the ball between themselves.

As the players become more proficient, change to 3 v 1, 5 v 2 and finally 4 v 2, using a larger area for the larger groups. The immediate impression that the players should gain from such an exercise is that life is a lot less strenuous if you have possession and let the ball do the work, than it is for those who have to chase it from player to player.

---

### Tips

The key words here are **options**, **angles** and **triangles**.

The players need to appreciate that the player with the ball requires as many passing *options* as possible, and needs to be supported by a minimum of two other colleagues who position themselves at *angles* which, given the space constraints, allow a pass which has the minimum chance of being intercepted. The angle should be as wide as possible. In essence, the three players are each positioned at the corners of a *triangle*, with the opponent at the centre and the supporting players holding blind side positions.

---

*If two opponents attempt to dispossess the player it means that one less player is marked.*

*Now both players are being marked. The opponent nearest the ball has jockeyed the player so that he really only has one colleague to pass to, and he is now being marked.*

When the 4 v 1 session begins, a number of faults will quickly become noticeable. The major fault is usually that the supporting players will not move into open space to receive the ball, but instead remain stationary or too close to the piggy.

Confident players will automatically find space because they want the ball. The less con-fident tend to hide behind the defender so that they, the defender and the player with the ball form a straight line. By their action, they effec-tively rule themselves out of the exercise. For the less confident, explain what they are doing wrong and if they persist, place them into a separate group of players, all of whom have the same problem. Provide them with additional sessions and special attention as the ability to move into space is vital if they are to progress.

Players are free to dribble with the ball, but invariably they dribble themselves into trouble. It is best if they concentrate on accurate passing, asking for periods of two-touch passing will assist in eradicating this problem

The main aim of the piggy is to close down the player with the ball as soon as possible so that they drop their heads and are forced into making errors. This is a fundamental defensive technique that they should use in any type of game.

*A successful pass is unlikely unless the player moves into space and provides his colleague with an angle and an option.*

*Now that he has moved, a successful pass is much more likely to occur.*

**Tips**

These exercises are hard work and initially should last for no longer than one minute, after which time the 'piggy' is changed. Swap the players on a regular basis as being 'piggy' should not be seen as a punishment posting. If you insist that the passer of the ball which is intercepted has to become the piggy, then the poorer players are likely to carry the brunt of the work and show little improvement.

*The player has moved into a good position to receive the pass.*

*The pass is made and the player moves forward, behind the defender, on his way to receive the ball.*

*He is now in free space and the ball is passed to him.*

Once there are at least two 'piggies', time can be spent explaining how they should work together so that one goes for the ball while the other covers the likely recipient of the pass. This technique of jockeying and providing support play is covered in a later chapter, and this exercise can be a good way of using it in a training situation. Certainly the tendency for young players to swamp an attacker and leave other players unmarked needs to be corrected as soon as possible.

Finally, the whole of the squad can be involved by dividing them into three equal teams in a large area and pitting one against two.

### Passing Across the Box

The objective is for the Green team to pass the ball continuously back and forth *across the box* via the two players inside the box.

The main points to emphasize are as follows:

### Attackers
- Initially keep well apart, spread the defence and keep moving in front of the ball.
- Try to stand side on as much as possible thereby making it easier to evade a defender.
- Move into space on the blind side wherever possible.

### Defenders
- Quickly mark a player, keeping an eye on both them and the ball.
- Endeavour to prevent a player turning.
- Immediately pressurize or close down the player with the ball.

The area should commence at 15 x 15m, and expand as the number of players increases. Develop the exercise in stages.

*Four Greens and One Red*

The game commences with a pass from a Green player outside the playing area. The two Green players in the middle can pass to each other, or pass back, as many times as the coach requires – three is a good minimum starting point.

Do not progress too quickly to the next stage – there needs to be a consistently good level of play achieved by the majority of the

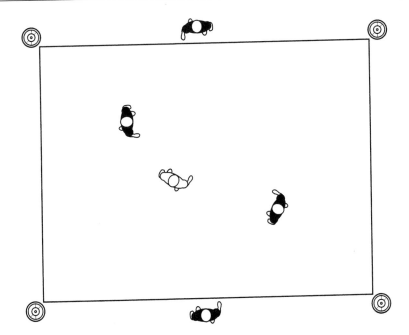

*Four Greens and one Red.*

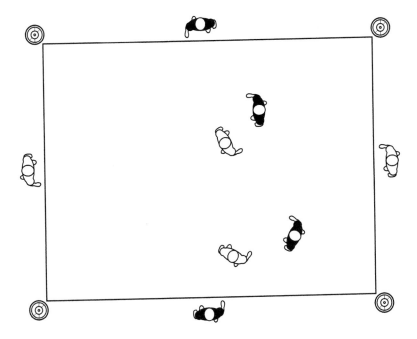

*Four Greens and four Reds.*

squad. Introduce two-touch play to add a level of difficulty.

*Four Greens and Two Reds*
Expand the area to 20 x 20m. The introduction of the extra Red adds a new level of difficulty to the exercise. The requirement for a minimum number of passes is now no longer necessary.

*Four Greens and Four Reds*
If the Greens lose possession, then the Reds have to pass the ball to either of their colleagues outside the playing area and maintain this play until dispossessed. The players outside the playing area must not remain stationary and wait for the ball to come straight to their feet. They should be constantly moving along the edge of the area so as to react quickly and offer the greatest assistance their colleagues. They must talk to their colleagues.

If possession is lost then it is essential for that team to pressure the opposition as quickly as possible. You can alternate commencement of the game between the Reds and Greens.

*Five Greens and Five Reds*
Expand the practice area to 30 x 30m and play as before.

# CHAPTER 9

# Defending

The coaching of defending techniques is a more difficult task than teaching attacking play. Attack has speed and excitement aimed towards a definite object, ideally a goal or a good shot at goal. Defending has greater subtleties; attacks by the opposition can simply be stifled by good positioning, a vital component of a defender's repertoire, but this is not the kind of activity that is seen by spectators as the essence of football. Good fullbacks are worth their weight in gold, but they never attract the praise given to the goalscorer.

It cannot be emphasized enough to the whole team that the defender's role is one that requires considerable skill. Booting the ball into touch or high into the opponent's half, which is how many defenders spend their time, is simply not good enough. Defenders have to track attackers, dispossess them of the ball and then initiate the start of an attack. This requires positioning and ball skills of the highest order and acquisition of those skills needs to start now.

It also needs to be stressed that when the team have lost possession, then to varying degrees, *the whole team have to become defenders*. Both attackers and midfield need to play their part, rather than stand and wait for somebody else to regain possession.

It doesn't matter how well the back three or four are organized, they will be at a severe disadvantage if the opposition's midfield is allowed plenty of time to play accurate through balls to their forward line. Midfield players will therefore need to mark their opposite number as part of the defending process.

## SUPPORTING PLAY

A major component of defending is support play, which in its simplest form should be considered as the second line of defence to ensure that potential 1 v 1 situations always become 2 v 1.

The objective is for defenders to 'slide' across the pitch to concentrate around the area of play. This means that some attackers on the opposite side from play are left relatively free while greater attention is given to their colleagues who are closer to the point of play. The concentration of defenders allows them to provide cover for their colleagues and act as a second line of defence.

Defenders have to develop an ability to position themselves so that they can see the player with the ball and also the position of the likely receiver of a possible pass. Of course, at some stage they will have to take action, either by moving closer to the possible receiver of the ball or closing in on the attacker with the ball.

Alas, junior players tend to do things in extremes. The concept of 'sliding' is difficult to grasp and they either remain strung out across the pitch in vulnerable positions or they over-concentrate their attentions on one player. One player being smothered by four defenders is not an uncommon sight.

## Jockeying the Opponent Away from the Goal

Use an area 40 x 10m. You will need such an area so that a realistic situation can be achieved in which the attacker makes a spirited run towards the defender.

In a one-on-one situation the attacker holds the initiative and to redress this imbalance defenders have to use their positioning skills. Use an assistant and initially walk through this exercise:

- attacker with ball runs in free space towards the defender;
- the defender moves forward as quickly as possible and tackles, or
- slows down, turns sideways and moves slightly off line towards the centre of the pitch.

A common mistake made by players is to run both directly towards and up to the attacker, as though to block their progress. A skilled attacker is likely to evade this kind of challenge and run on unimpeded, leaving the defender stranded. The defender should therefore attempt to take a curved run towards the opponent, gradually slowing down and moving 'off centre', leaving some distance between themselves and the attacker.

The defender should be sideways on, the purpose of which is that it makes it easier to accelerate forward alongside the attacker. Moving 'off centre' opens a gap between the touchline and the defender. In such situations the attacker will momentarily slow down so as to assess the situation, and then most likely go for the gap. In doing so, they begin to lose the initiative.

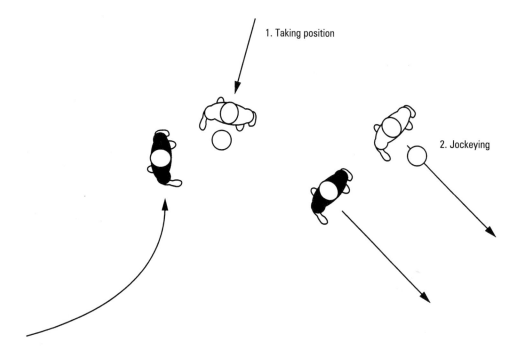

1. Taking position

2. Jockeying

*Jockeying techniques.*

*The defender moves towards the advancing attacker.*

*He now turns side-on and off-centre so as to jockey the attacker in the desired direction.*

As the attacker goes for the gap, the defender now changes direction and accelerates to run parallel with them, narrowing the gap and pushing or 'jockeying' the attacker into the corner areas or along the touchline. Defenders must keep their eyes on the ball at all times, and at the appropriate moment, make a tackle. Even if they chose not to tackle, they will have slowed down the advance, placed the attacker in an inferior situation, and bought time for both themselves and the rest of the defence to strengthen their positions.

*He moves in close, running parallel with the attacker, keeping an eye on the ball at all times, seeking an opportunity to tackle.*

| Tips |
| --- |
| A good way to instil the technique of jockeying players is to insist that it is used in small-sided games with no tackling allowed. |

If the attacker attempts to move towards the centre of the pitch the defender also moves back in the same direction, ensuring that the gap, and thus the desired channel for the attacker's run, is always maintained.

When defending while the ball is near to, or in the penalty area, the defender must never:

- Defend backwards into their own penalty area – in such a situation the defender must quickly go straight for the ball.
- Attempt to dribble the ball to safety – either pass it out to the wings or kick it into touch.
- Pass the ball across the mouth of the goal.

### Right- and Left-Footed Players

Most players are likely to be right-footed. Defenders should quickly recognize whether the players they are marking are left- or right-footed because that will be the side their opponents are more confident in moving towards.

A left-footed player on the left wing only has to run *around* the defender in order to get the angle to make a cross. A right-footed player on the *left* wing, unless they are very fast, will always need to move *inside* the defender to cross the ball. Defenders on the right side of the team should therefore watch for the opposition trying to cut inside.

### Positioning

As a general rule, defenders need to mark by ensuring that they stand *between* the opposition player and their goal, astride an imaginary line which is drawn from the opponent through to the centre of their goal. This is the same line that goalkeepers should be astride in order to narrow the angle.

### Support Play Exercise

Support play is not an easy concept for young players to grasp and you should not expect too much from them at this age. For this exercise, you will need an area 20 x 15m. Use three players on each team. The objective is for team B to take the ball across team A's line:

- The practice commences by A1 passing to B1 and initially follows the 'jockeying' exercise.
- As A1 runs towards B1, A2 and A3 cover B2 and B3.

As a general rule:

- The greater the pressure exerted on B1 by A1, and therefore the less options available, the tighter the marking can be by the supporting players.

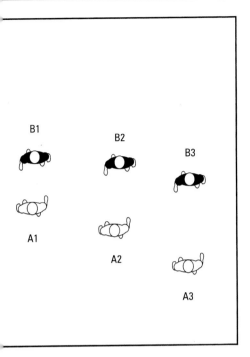

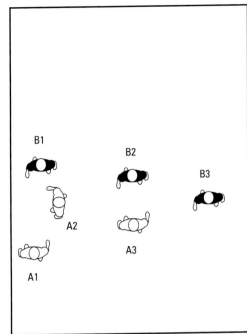

*First contact.*

*Supporting position.*

the support players should adopt a 'line astern' approach so that each player covers the player ahead, marking space *and* keeping an eye on the movements of their immediate opponent.

As A1 moves towards B1, A2 moves to provide cover as A3 moves to cover B2. This leaves B3 relatively free, but the chances of this player receiving the ball are now considerably reduced.

# CHAPTER 10

# Goalkeeping

The first requirement is to find a player with a strong desire to be a goalkeeper – that is, someone who will perform the most acrobatic of saves into deep mud or onto a hard, frozen ground without a moment's hesitation.

Goalkeepers need to be reliable, slightly mad, brave, and as tall and agile as possible with a good kick. They also need to be a forceful and confident character to take command of the defence in free kick and corner situations.

In many matches, a goalkeeper may only touch the ball ten or fifteen times, and the goals that are scored are not usually the result of lack of agility on their part but more frequently due to:

- Poor positioning.
- Basic ball-handling deficiencies.
- Poor defending by their colleagues.
- Taking their eyes off the ball, or more specifically closing their eyes once the ball has been kicked towards them, particularly at close range (closing the eyes is an automatic response by the body when under attack, but by overriding the response the goalkeeper has a better chance to react more positively).

Goalkeeper training requires one-to-one sessions, which is difficult to achieve if you have no assistants to help you. If it is possible for the player to attend a specialist goal keeping course, then this should certainly be encouraged.

## GENERAL AGILITY SKILLS

- Ball thrown at or to the side of the goal keeper who has to catch ball while:

  - sitting upright with legs out straight;
  - on both knees;
  - squatting.

The ball is thrown at a variety of speeds and angles to make the goalkeeper both stretch and move to collect the ball. Some balls should be short so that the goalkeeper moves forward and others long so that they must move back wards.

- Ground balls are rolled and then kicked in along the ground. The main point of this is to ensure that the goalkeeper gets both hands and legs behind the ball and then cradles it in their chest. The legs act as the second line of defence should the ball slip through the hands
- Chest high balls are thrown in.
- High balls are both thrown in with the goalkeeper leaping and catching it with both hands. It should be a running leap off one leg. The hands must be pointing upward and the thumbs touching.

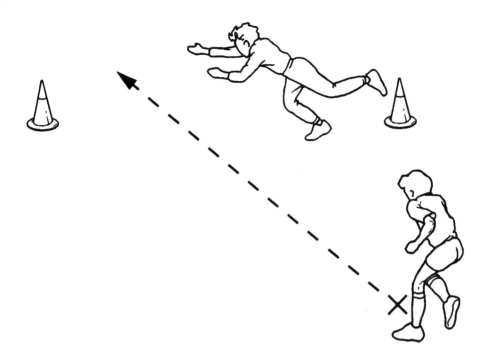

*Diving exercise.*

In these exercises, the goalkeeper must constantly be moving sideways on the balls of their feet and always facing the ball. They should not run sideways for they will find it difficult to get both hands behind the ball and their body cannot act as a second line of defence.

- Have the goalkeeper face you with their legs wide apart. Roll the ball between their legs so that once it has passed between them they have to turn and secure the ball.
- Have the goalkeeper stand with their back towards you. Throw the ball towards them at a variety of angles and speed. As the ball leaves your hands shout out the word 'turn' so that they can turn, take sight of the ball and collect it.

- Set up the two cones and position the goalkeeper at one cone. Pass the ball towards the other cone and as you make contact with the ball the goalkeeper should then *move sideways on their toes* and dive to collect the ball. One hand should be behind the ball and the other on top.
- Time should be spent in undertaking the defence of corner kicks. Goalkeepers must have a good understanding of what is trying to be achieved so that they can take command of their six-yard box and insist that players mark the opposition.

Goalkeepers also let themselves down by poor positioning. The two major faults are:

- Standing on the line when they should move out.

*Continuous shooting exercise.*

- Not understanding the concept of narrowing the angle.

To a large extent the two faults are linked together. The shooting exercises are an excellent way to coach goalkeepers in these two techniques:

- Set up three cones and three players with three balls providing a variety of shots at the goalkeeper. The goalkeeper must be ready before each shot is taken otherwise the exercise is devalued.

# CHAPTER 11

# Small-Sided Games

## THE SMALL-SIDED GAME IN YOUTH FOOTBALL

### The Importance of Small-Sided Games

Small-sided games are a vital part of training. To add substance to this assertion, below is a summary of a German study* undertaken to find ways to make youth football more attractive. The study compared players of –10 years playing 11 v 11 football on a reduced full-size pitch, 7 v 7 on a half field and 7 v 7 on a 35 ˇ 55yd pitch. A summary of the results is as follows:

The 11 v 11 game was essentially an endurance test with limited ball possession and dominated by a few talented players. In 50 minutes each player ran an average distance of 4,236 yards, only 1,000 yards less than a Bundesliga player. The attackers were in possession of the ball for three-quarters of the time, the defenders presumably 'booting it' anywhere as soon as they made contact.

The Teutonic thoroughness of the study is not in doubt but this average distance equates to two and a half miles, which seems quite un-believable for a ten-year-old. No wonder they soon run out of steam.

- In the 7 v 7 game on a half field, the pitch was still too big. It resulted in uneven distribution of the ball, little midfield play, long kicks into the opposition third and most goals being scored as the result of solo efforts. Sounds familiar?
- The 7 v 7 on a 35 x 55yd pitch allowed all players to come into regular and frequent contact with the ball. There were more goals scored than in the other two games and all players had a greater opportunity to practise basic skills.
- Lastly the study looked at 4 v 4 games on a 30 x 20yd pitch. The conclusion was that this led to even more confidence in ball handling skills and shots on goal.

Small games allow players to touch the ball much more frequently and consequently be far more confident and involved in the game. In a full-sized game, it is quite possible for a player to go through an entire session and never touch the ball. Not so much football as a new version of jogging!

It needs to be stressed that it will be of benefit to all of the players if they can appreciate that defenders need to be as skilful as attackers. Unfortunately, the Under 10 caste system frequently means that attackers are the 'glory boys' whilst the clumsy and the slow finish up

As reported in *The Yorkshire Post* (27 January 1999). The information was drawn from a collaboration between the German Soccer Federation and the University of Cologne.

at the back. Defenders seem to be chosen because of their physique, rather than their skill.

Small games provide an excellent opportunity for defenders to develop the skills of obtaining the ball, maintaining possession and then building up attacks. One of these areas is the ability for a ball to be passed by a goalkeeper to a defender for an attack to be initiated.

Good small-sided games players are invariably good players in what ever size of team they play. Therefore the standard achieved when playing these games is a good indicator of what the potential would be as a full-sized team.

It is suggested that you start with 2 v 2 and then slowly build up both in the size of the teams and the pitch, as the proficiency improves.

Such games should be used to practise the techniques which the players have acquired in the earlier part of the session. There should be a clear link between the two sets of activities otherwise little progress will be made. The accent should be on the improvement of the individual player and their ability to grasp fully the basic techniques and skills of the game. This means that the final score is of lesser importance than trying to utilize those exercises. This is not a concept which youngsters find easy to accept . . . and nor do many coaches.

### The Needs of Different Age Groups

Managers need to appreciate that different age groups show different characteristics in their approach to playing football and they should tailor their use of small-sided games accordingly.

A player aged less than nine who is in possession of the ball will run with their head down, eyes on the ball, no clear sense of direction and will be surrounded by colleagues who have come to provide some kind of assistance, though they are uncertain as to what it will be. Players at this age will tackle but with a view to dispossess, not necessarily to regain possession. The concepts of marking and team shape simply do not exist. Games should be limited to a maximum of 3 v 3.

A player aged from 9–11 years will be less selfish and begin to look for passing options but is still unlikely to move with any deliberation into space. The concept of attack, midfield and defence begins to take shape as does the need to mark, albeit somewhat erratically. Players will show a greater sense of anticipation of events and begin to understand the need to maintain possession. Games should be limited to a maximum of 5 v 5.

Players aged twelve and over will begin to work as a unit with a growing sense of tactical awareness. There will be an overall improvement in all areas of their game and the concept of consistently working together as a team will emerge. Attack and defence have a consistency of shape but the midfield is often the weak link, as it tends to disappear from sight. Games should be limited to a maximum of 7 v 7.

### Imposing Conditions of Play

To speed the development of a better style of play, conditions should be sparingly imposed upon the way a session is played. Conditions should be used to improve deficiencies, not to reduce better skills and techniques. For example, frequent use of limited touch football is likely to have a negative effect upon the acquisition of dribbling skills or running with the ball.

The wisdom of these conditions is not always appreciated by the players and it should be explained to them what is the object of the exercise. It is better to alternate often during a session between open and conditioned play so as the improvement in performance can be seen.

Games should quickly progress to be played with *two-touch passing*. This encourages good first touch, ball control and accurate passing. *Below head height* play can also be introduced in addition to two-touch passing, or as a single condition. Penalize sides by awarding their opponents half a goal each time the ball goes above head height in a deliberate as opposed to an accidental manner. Ideally, players should progress to *one-touch* football, but this may be asking too much at such a young age.

Imposing these conditions forces players to find and create space, minimizes wild kicks into orbit and the development of 'aerial ping-pong'.

Another condition to impose is possession football. Players must appreciate that maintaining possession of the ball is absolutely vital as it allows the pace, timing and direction of play to be dictated with some degree of certainty.

Once one side has scored they now have to keep possession until the other side scores, in which case the situation is now reversed. The term 'possession football' is often interpreted to indicate that it is an exercise to be undertaken and when completed the players go back to 'normal' football. Normal football in this context would seem to consist of giving the ball away to the opposition as soon as possible, a case of 'dispossession football'.

Possession football is not 'showboating', nor is it stringing a number of passes together for the sake of passing, nor does it matter whether the passes are long, short, fast or slow. It means that the team accepting responsibility for moving the ball forward to realistic shooting opportunities in a manner which minimizes the threat of dispossession. A team cannot score if they do not have the ball, and therefore when they have it, they need to keep it.

Small games allow players to appreciate that when possession is lost, then to varying degrees *all* of the team become *defenders*, and when possession is gained, then to varying degrees *all* of the team become *attackers*.

## Essentials of Small Game Coaching

Before you commence, tell the teams that you will concentrate on coaching one team on one specific topic, such as creating space, for a limited period and then you will turn your attention to the other team and deal with another topic. This keeps both teams motivated and avoids accusations of favouritism. If you try to correct all of the huge catalogue of errors that both teams make, as they occur in a random fashion, it is highly likely that you will find yourself making little overall improvement.

Initially, concentrate on major mistakes only, dealing with them one at a time. As so much is likely to be wrong, too much intervention would result in minimal playing time.

Make generous use of the game that youngsters know as 'statues'. When the whistle is blow all of the players have to stop moving immediately and 'freeze' in position. As many of them will be stationary anyway this should not be too hard to achieve. Use this game when mistakes are about to or have taken place. Once they have stopped moving, explain the error, demonstrate the options available which could rectify the situation, and then allow the game to recommence.

Many players, particularly older ones, who have not been used to these stoppages in play, will resist their use. Do not be discouraged by this – keep forcing the issue until the benefits to individual players become apparent.

Take the example of coaching how to create space. In the game the player running with the ball along the touchline allows themselves to be 'jockeyed' into the opposition corner and gives away a goal kick. When that occurs, stop play and reconstruct the events leading up to the loss of possession. Demonstrate what options were available. These could be:

- keep running and force a corner – high-risk option
- outpace the defender – unlikely
- pass the ball forward – no-one forward to receive
- cross the ball – likely to be blocked by defender
- cut inside the defender – possible option
- turn to find space – probably the best option. What type of turn would be best? What would the player do in the space? Pass to a colleague, but where are they? Pass and then move into a position to receive? Which position, ahead or to the side?

Examine the options, agree with the player on a new course of action and then allow play to restart.

## The Essentials of Attacking Play

The essentials of attack to concentrate upon using a 2–1–2 formation in a six-a-side game are as follows:

- Stretch the defence to create space by making the players disperse throughout the width and depth of the pitch.

Young players, because of the basic 'herd' instinct, still tend to mass in a group and therefore find dispersing over the pitch slightly alien. Attaining width anywhere on the pitch seems to be the greatest problem, one that it is possibly reinforced by the instructions of managers to get the ball to the star player, usually the striker, as soon as possible. This results in the ball going straight down the middle to the striker around the halfway line, or as so often happens, they come back to get the ball and set off for a solo dribbling run.

Young players seem to be encouraged to

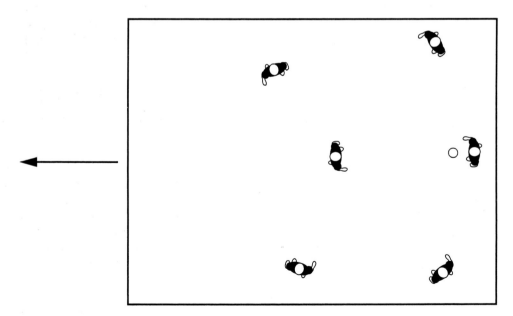

*2–1–2 formation.*

run straight into the opposition rather than use the less congested space of the touch-lines.

- Encourage players to adopt an open stance, usually side on, so as to have the widest field of vision of play. The emphasis should be on a good first touch, as it may be the only opportunity that occurs when the ball comes to them.
- Other players must find space and move in front of the ball, seeking blind side positions wherever possible to receive a pass.

Players should try to play the way they face. If they have their backs to the opposition's goal, then they need support *behind the ball*, so that they can pass and then move into space. If the support is not immediately forthcoming, then their priority must be to retain possession by placing their body between the opposition and the ball. If they are facing the opposition's goal then they need support in front of the ball. Such passes into space should be on the basis of creating space and delivering the ball as the player arrives, rather than the player arriving and waiting for the ball.

- The objective of the pass should be to cause the opposition problems, not to get the attacker out of trouble. Don't allow the opposition time to close down the player with the ball.

Unless a player shows a consistent ability to pass a defender, it may a better approach for them to pass the ball as soon as they come within a few metres of the opposition. They may have the initiative, but it is highly likely that they will lose this advantage if they find themselves in a blocking or tack-ling situation.

- Make passes, preferably to players behind an opponent, to move the ball quickly forward into the attacking half of the pitch.

- Pass and then move into a more advanta-geous position so as to take a shot at goal, receive a good pass in return or to draw an opponent.
- Get the attacking side to compress together in a more compact shape *en bloc* once the direction of play has been established so as to provide continuous close support for short, rapid passing.

The example on page 72 (top) shows how the team moves together to provide support and lessen passing distances. Note how the goalkeeper has also moved up the field to receive passes and redistribute the ball.

Once the team is using the width of the pitch there is a tendency to remain in such positions. Players who remain on the far side of the pitch are effectively out of the game. They will say that they are waiting for a pass, but the distances involved and the accuracy required, particularly if the ball is being played below head height, mean that this is highly unlikely to occur. They are waiting for a train that will never arrive.

An example of what usually happens is shown on page 72 (bottom).

### The Essentials of Defending Play

The essentials of defence to concentrate upon are:

- Keep the opposition in their half as long as possible by moving up the pitch and compressing the area of play. Forwards need to close down defenders as it is easier to score by dispossessing them on the edge of *their* penalty area than your defenders dispossessing their attackers on the edge of *your* penalty area.
- All players should initially mark on a one-to-one basis. This is particularly relevant for youngsters as they find this easier to grasp

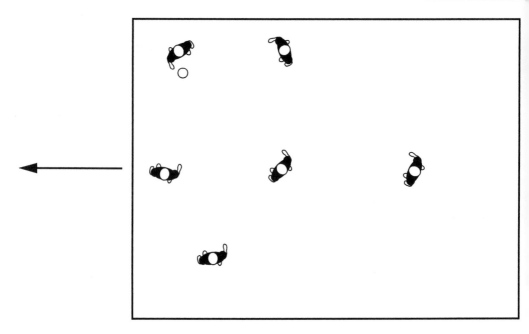

*Compact supporting play.*

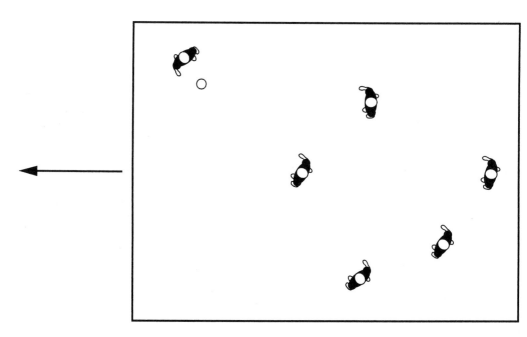

*Poor supporting play.*

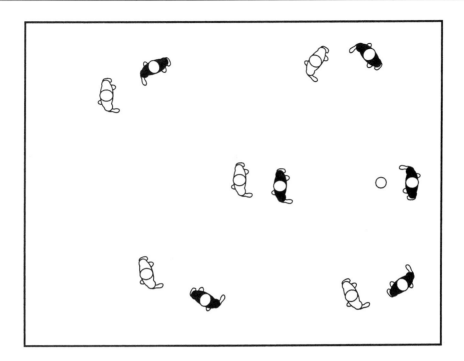

*Attacking and defending formation.*

than the often elusive concept of marking space.

The rule of thumb is that the further you are away from the ball the more you mark both the man and space, allowing greater leeway between yourself and the opposing player, so that you have a greater range of options, a large field of vision and are not overly committed to one course of action. The position at kick-off would be as shown above.

- Compress play around the player with the ball to force errors, reduce options and intercept passes. Quickly identify those opposition players who have poor ball skills and can easily be forced into making expensive errors.
- Quickly cover the ground and put pressure on the player with the ball, forcing them to

look to their feet and so restricting their field of vision.

- Tackle immediately, or go side-on and jockey them down the line or into the

| Tips |
|------|
| One way to get these ideas across to players is to work within a very small area and 'walk' them through the game, explaining what is required and why it is necessary.<br><br>Don't select two captains and let them choose their teams as it becomes a long-winded process when time is at a premium. Quickly choose the two sides so that they are as balanced as possible, tell them what the session is about and get them playing as soon as possible. |

centre of play. Provide support to colleagues who are attempting to close down or jockey an opponent.

- At all times keep goalside of the player being marked, and wherever possible, prevent them turning.
- As a defender be patient, keep balanced and on your feet, with your eye on the ball.
- When the ball is regained, keep possession. Let the ball do the work. The ball will not tire but the opposition will. Wear out and frustrate the opposition as they chase the ball. Move the ball as quickly as possible into the opponent's half, but at a rate which minimizes the risk of dispossession.

In both attack and defence the aim should be to outnumber the opposition, so giving weight to the saying that the winners are usually those 'that get there the fastest with the mostest'.

Finally, on the subject of passing, it is usually forgotten that it is the player without the ball that makes the play. Unless the player without the ball moves into an advantageous position to receive the ball, then the passing skills of the player with the ball, however accurate, are largely wasted.

Conventional wisdom says that coaching should take place from the touchlines. However, you may reap greater rewards by playing and by showing the teams how it should be

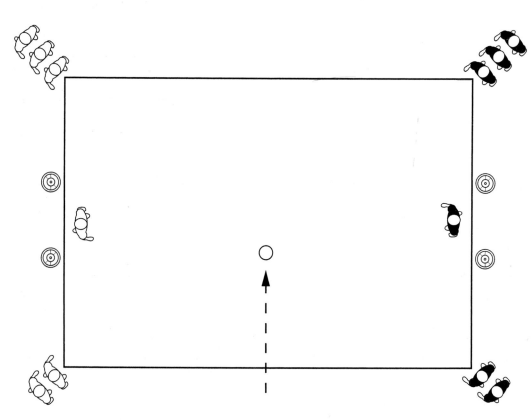

*Small-sided game 1.*

done. Limit yourself to two-tap, don't show off and remember that as a coach you are not allowed to score goals . . . unless of course you get desperate!

## EXAMPLE GAMES

### Small-Sided Games 1

*2 v 2, 3 v 3*

- Use an area of 20 x 30m.
- Use permanent goalkeepers throughout the session.
- Use wide goals to encourage scoring.
- Organize two teams and allocate players into the corners.
- Blow the whistle and kick the ball into the centre, whereupon *one* player from each corner runs simultaneously into the arena in order to obtain possession and score.
- Play continues until a goal is scored, the ball goes out of play or the set time period is reached.
- Players must then leave the pitch and a new game starts.
- If the number of players in each corner is kept unequal, then as the players rotate they will play with a different colleague and be exposed to a different standard of support. When playing 3 v 3, add the third group of players around a cone located by the side of the goals.

### Small-Sided Games 2

*4 v 4, 5 v 5, 6 v 6, 7 v 7*

- Use an area of between 60 x 40m to 30 x 20m depending upon the number of players.
- For the larger area, divide the pitch into three thirds so that offside can be played, otherwise 'goal hanging' becomes the norm.

---

**Tips**

Unbalance the sides by confining two defenders and three attackers to each half. This encourages the defenders to get the ball into the opposition's half as soon as possible.

---

- The goals should be wide so as to encourage shots.
- To give 'shape' to the team, use a 2–2 formation for 5 v 5 and 2–1–2 for 6 v 6.
- Allow a few minutes of free play so that the team can demonstrate that they have forgotten most of what they were taught the previous week.

  Playing possession football can be a good way to commence the session. Impose the condition that the players cannot return the ball directly back to the passer of the ball – as this will necessitate greater movement by the players.

- Play should commence in a number of ways:

  - the ball is rolled out by the goalkeeper;
  - by a throw-in;
  - the coach kicks in from the sideline.

- Choose one aspect of play to coach and coach only one side at a time.

  It is not only better to choose one aspect of play, such as attacking, but to sub-divide it and concentrate on one of the individual factors such as achieving width. This 'building blocks' approach may seem slow, but it will achieve greater results in the long run.

Take care when telling players to 'hold up' or 'mark tight', or similar terms, unless you have explained and demonstrated what you require.

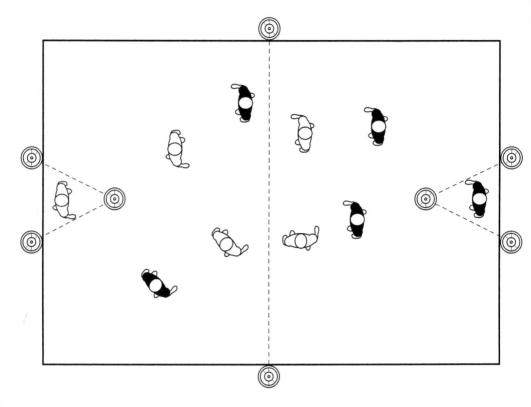

*Small-sided game 2.*

Don't *assume* that they know what you mean.

It is better to play unlimited touches of the ball for the first few minutes, then change to a maximum of three-touch and then two-touch. You should see an immediate improvement in play with the change to two-tap as the teams become more compact in an effort to create space and provide support. Return to un-limited touches at regular intervals.

## Small-Sided Games 3

*4 v 4, 5 v 5, 6 v 6, 7 v 7*

With young players there is some merit in dividing the pitch by its length so that they can be taught when to spread and when to compress play:

- Use an area of between 55 x 35m to 30 x 20m depending upon the number of players.
- The triangular area is only for the goal-keeper.
- Split each team in half and ensure that they stay in their designated half.
- The goalkeeper *rolls* out the ball to a defender so that an attack can commence.

The pitch can also be divided into three equal zones, as opposed to two, and the players allocated in pairs to each area. The ball

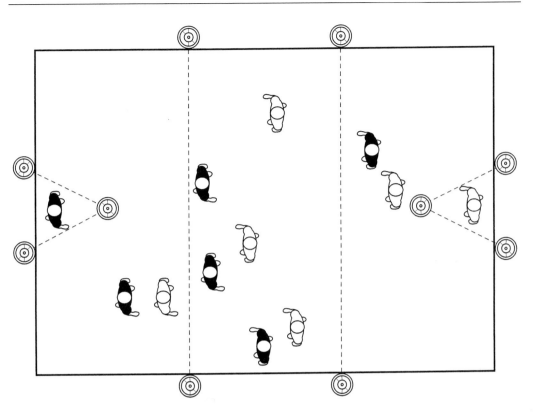

*Small-sided game 3.*

must be played through, not over the middle zone.

The division of the pitch into three areas provides an excellent way for the players to begin to appreciate how a defence, mid-field and attack can both develop as separate units and work together. It also opens up a number of opportunities to place players into different match situations:

- To alter the spread of players so that the ends become more crowded and the middle third has only one pair, and vice versa.

  When the end areas have only one pair then the other players can enter these spaces

but only after the ball has entered the area.
- To alter the conditions of play. Examples would be:

  – the ends are confined to one-tap play in order to hone quick shooting and ball clearance skills;
  – a goal will not count until all of the team, except the goalkeeper, are in the middle or attacking thirds of the pitch. This encourages compact play and helps to prevent the gaping midfield gap that is so prevalent with youngsters;
  – introduce offside to hinder 'goal hanging' and develop the use of through balls;

– pair off opposing players so that they are left in no doubt who they have to mark throughout the session on all areas of the pitch. This is an arduous exercise, but it drives home the benefits of tight marking.

## Small-Sided Games 4

This variation is very useful for emphasizing:

- the importance of support play and the defenders sliding across the pitch to where the ball is being played;
- attackers making use of blind-side runs and receiving diagonal balls which split the defence.

Initially it should be set up as follows:

- Use an area of at least 40 x 30m, excluding the area behind the goal.
- Use four attackers, three defenders, one ball retriever and one goalkeeper, increase to four defenders as the attack becomes more proficient.
- Keep the goal wide to encourage shots, which should be taken at every opportunity.
- The attackers start the game at the end opposite to the goal from a stationary ball on the line.
- Alternate between open play and the ball being kept below head height.
- Play throw-ins but not corners.
- The defenders have to dispossess the attackers and place the ball between cones in the opposition's corners. The game then restarts.

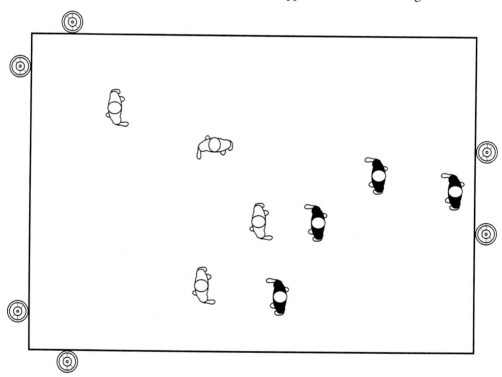

*Small-sided game 4.*

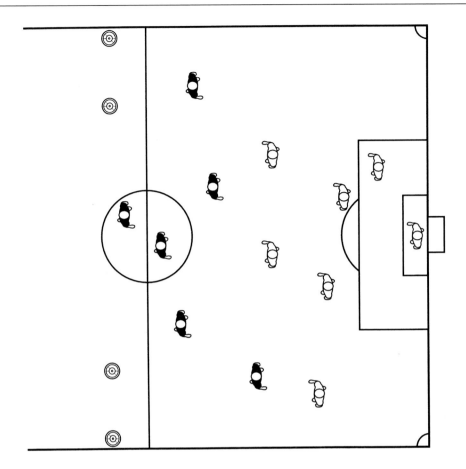

*Small-sided game 5.*

## Small-Sided Games 5

This is a very useful exercise to practise free kicks, corners, throwing and goal kicks, as well as different playing combinations of players who constitute the defence and attack:

- Use the whole of a full-size pitch.
- Define which positions constitute both the defence and attack.
- The defence has to stay in its own half *at all times*.
- The attack starts the play in its own half

and moves towards the opposition.

- The defence has to dispossess and score goals by passing the ball through either set of small cones but without leaving its half of the field.
- Once the ball has passed over the halfway line the defence reorganize in readiness for another attack.
- As the defence gets better, narrow the two goals and place them further into the attacking half.
- Also practise sending in high balls from the opposing half so as to test the defence.

## SET PIECES

### Free Kicks

Set pieces present an opportunity to place players in advantageous situations which would not be available in normal play. For example, it would not be usual to have seven players in the opposition's penalty area, but this could be achieved when a free kick is being taken on the edge of the box.

The problem is that free kicks do not occur very often in junior football and thought needs to be given to how much time should be spent on such practice, when it could be used to better benefit on more basic exercises. Perhaps using the player with the hardest and most accurate shot will suffice in most situations.

Players need to determine whether the free kick is direct or indirect, and take it quickly to maintain the advantage. The rules state that the ball should be stationary before the kick is taken. If the kick is direct and positioned close to the edge of the penalty area, then a shot at goal is a good option. If the opposition players are forming a wall they must be 10yds from the ball. This may be the only time that you wait to take a free kick.

### Corners

You may not have the most skilful team on the day, but you can have the most organized, and this is very important when taking corners. All players should know precisely what

---

**Tips**

Check with the referee before the game whether set kicks of all kinds can be taken quickly or whether the players need to wait for the whistle.

---

responsibilities they have when defending or taking a corner.

When a corner has been awarded against your team the players must quickly go to their allotted positions, keeping their eyes on the ball at all times. It is not unknown for teams to walk towards their goal with their backs towards the corner as the ball sails over their heads and into the goal.

If the opposition looks about to play a short corner, then two players should quickly go to cover the situation; one player is likely be outmanoeuvred by the two opponents. Two players should cover the posts and so give greater freedom to the goalkeeper. Covering the posts does not mean leaning on them as though to gently fall asleep, but rather standing on the line an arm's length in from the posts looking at the ball.

The goalkeeper should be just off his line and slightly nearer to the rear goalpost. This is because it is easier to come forward for a ball from the rear post than it is to go backwards for a ball when near the front post. The goalkeeper should be the king of the 6-yard box and making sure that all of the opposition are well marked.

When playing a corner the tactics you use will be determined by whether you have players who have the ability to deliver a consistently accurate corner kick. If possible, the ball should drop between the 6-yard box and the penalty spot, so making it difficult for the goalkeeper to come out to collect the ball.

One player should mark the goalkeeper and another should be at the back post to catch the ball that invariably passes straight through the throng of bodies. All of the other players should be out in the penalty area and move in as the kick is taken.

Only use short corners if you have players who do not have a sufficiently good kick or you are playing on a very large pitch. If you must take a short corner then ensure that the two players involved fully understand what they have to do, especially the need to take it quickly.

## Goal Kicks

When young players are on an oversized pitch, managers should agree that placed goal kicks should be taken from the edge of the penalty area. This prevents the problem of weak kicks barely reaching the edge of the penalty area when taken in the conventional way.

The biggest problem that occurs with placed goal kicks is your team standing still and watching the ball go straight to an opponent. Make sure that the team spread across the pitch so as to stretch the opposition, and that players move quickly towards the ball. Also instruct the goalkeeper to aim for the point where the halfway line meets the touchline. This increases the distance to the goal in the event of dispossession.

## Offside

There is no offside in small-sided games, and good teams usually have few problems adjusting to offside when they first play with eleven players. Make sure that they are aware of what constitutes being offside and how they cannot be offside from a corner, a throw-in or a goalkick.

Conventional wisdom would say that the defenders should move out from goal and up the pitch to place the opposing attackers in an offside position. This is far easier said than done, and it takes some experience and confidence for a back four to move out in a disciplined manner. Even professionals have problems achieving this, so perhaps it is asking too much of youngsters. It also assumes that if they do so the referee will pick up the offside players but that may well not happen.

Perhaps a better solution in the first instance would be to make sure that the players mark the opposition and leave the moving out to when a high proficiency in marking has been achieved.

## TEAM FORMATION

### Team Positions

The official move towards small-sided games should eventually prove to be a very successful development. It needs to be extended to the older age groups, and there is a very good case for six- or seven-a-side games being continued up to the Under 14s level.

The resistance to small-sided games does not come from the players. Certainly there are considerable problems at club level in being able to use suitably sized pitches, and these kinds of practical issues do not seem to be receiving much in-depth consideration by the footballing authorities. However, real resistance to this change comes from the managers, and it is difficult to come to a conclusion other than the fact that many managers do not see small-sided games as real football. Large-sided games provide them with the opportunity to play 'big time' and adopt established player formations such as 4–4–2. But it is doubtful that managers fully understand what such formations are meant to achieve or that the young players understand what they are supposed to do. When managers say that their team is ready for full-sized games, what they probably mean is that it is they who want to upgrade the size of play.

If the techniques and skills of a team are poor, then managers are likely to be deluding both themselves and the players if they believe that concentrating on 4–4–2 or 3–5–2, or any

81

It may be best to sort out the defence first and initially allow the attack to take care of itself. Good defences are the backbone of consistently good teams, breaking down the opposition and then recommencing attacks. A strong attack and a weak defence may make for initial success and excitement but in the long run the defence will prove to be the weak link.

other kind of formation for that matter, is going to make any appreciable difference to the quality of their play. It is more than likely that the only time the players follow the pattern it is at kick-off, and the rest of the time they play as a largely uncoordinated group. Commonsense would suggest that the system of play should be arranged to suit the available skills and not be a case of forcing players to follow a set pattern. Set patterns are likely to lead to set minds.

With youngsters there is considerable merit in discarding the notion of set team patterns, and simply concentrate on producing players who are comfortable to play in a variety of positions.

However, reality suggests that there has to be some kind of general framework within which the players initially work – and besides which, everybody has to stand somewhere! For that reason, a loose 4–3–3 formation is suggested, for the simple reason that it spreads the players throughout the pitch and seems to produce a more balanced side.

If possible, one of the central defenders operates behind the back three acting as a kind of last resort to provide support and push the defence up the field so as to avoid the large midfield gap which often occurs. It does take a special kind of player to undertake the 'last resort' role, someone who is intelligent, has elements of being able to read the game and

is capable of roaming from side to side. Such players are not always readily available, and when they are they invariably become the captain.

It seems easier to get across to players the virtues of a supportive 3–3–3 bloc moving, hopefully, as one unit around the pitch. Such a formation has a central backbone and three players on each side who are encouraged to use the wings. And that's it.

All players, particularly defenders, are encouraged to make runs forward, as tactically this is desirable, and they will only gain confidence when actually attempting to do so. However, although it is desirable that another player should take their place when they do so, it is being unrealistic to expect youngsters at this age to have such a degree of tactical awareness.

**Placing Players in Position**

Very quickly, you will notice the characteristics of the players and in your mind begin to formulate the framework you hopefully intend to use. Some are natural terriers, some good tacklers and very industrious, some 'goal hang', some hold back, some have a good touch to the ball, some are brave, others less so, some get to the edge of the penalty area and run out of ideas, some want to take on the whole opposition single-handedly, some talk a good game, and finally some . . . well, some just want to run around in a Manchester United shirt.

So from this rich human mix, for the initial matches players are asked where they want to play. The players are given a brief outline of the kind of characteristics and abilities that are required and then volunteers are requested. Most children seem to be able to place themselves with a high degree of accuracy in the position to which, at least initially, they feel they are best suited. In this way, they are encouraged to play in accordance with their natural temperament and inclinations.

Once the children are playing in the position of their choice then they are on your side, and if the result is not as successful as you or they would like then it is much easier to make the necessary adjustments. By their own standards they are usually only too aware of when they are not making the grade and will often ask to play in another position without this being suggested to them.

## Do You Want Them to Learn or to Win?

Well, of course the answer is that you want both, but it often doesn't work out like that. There has to be a constant need to experiment as players come and go or develop at different rates. Experimenting carries a degree of risk which equates to losing games. This may be the short-term price you have to pay for building up a successful squad in the long term.

# CHAPTER 12

# The Match

The big day has finally arrived. If you are lucky you may see glimpses, admittedly fairly brief glimpses, of some of the techniques and skills that you have undertaken in the training sessions. Be realistic about what the team can achieve.

The following is a reminder of some of the points to consider before, or on, the match day.

## BEFORE THE MATCH

### Nutrition

Parents need to be encouraged to ensure that their children have eaten suitable food no later than two hours before the start of the game. If they eat later then the digestive process will affect their energy levels. Ideally, they should be having some easily digestible high carbo-hydrate food such as bread, toast, porridge,

banana or cereals which can be converted into energy during the match. Some players seem to run out of steam quite quickly, and some of this situation must be as a result of having had no food since the previous evening.

### Pre-Match Day Organization

*Quick Checklist*

- Check colours of opponent's strip.
- confirm kick-off time
- confirm pitch location
- who will referee?
- make team selection
- confirm the name of the opponent's manager.

It is vital to check in advance the colour of the opponent's strip. Failure to do this results in the inevitable panic of trying to sort out some kind of last minute solution. Twenty players in near identical strip does not make for good football. The usual solution if this does occur is to turn the shirts of one team inside out.

The kick-off time should be agreed and made known to both players *and* parents. If the weather looks bad, the major problem usually being a frozen and icy pitch, then arrange for an inspection to be carried out early morning on the day of the game. Never take a risk. If a child's studs will not sink in, or there is ice on the pitch, then do not play. If it is likely to be cold make sure the players

---

**Tips**

There is no need to use sports drinks or those with high levels of caffeine. They are expensive, and their value is still a matter of debate. Tap water is perfectly adequate. Players should drink plenty of water up to about 30 minutes before kick-off. Dehydration sets in much quicker than people realize, and when you feel a need for liquids it is usually too late to compensate properly.

---

have tracksuit bottoms, hats and gloves to wear whilst playing. Remember that the substitutes will also be waiting in the cold and need to keep warm.

Tell the opposition your exact location if you are at home. It is not unknown for teams to go to the wrong pitch. If you are away, find out the opposition's exact location as it has been known for the entire convoy of parents to become collectively lost. You should also ascertain whether there are changing rooms. If not, where does everyone change?

You must establish whether a referee is required. If at all possible, do not referee your own game. Despite your protestations to the contrary, you will not only be biased towards one side or the other, but if your team is losing badly it is soul destroying to have to watch it from the centre. (If you really want to referee then attend a referee's training course to obtain your badge. This will usually take up one night a week for six weeks.)

Finally, choose the team. Issue selection slips at the end of the training session which show the time and date of the match, the place of meeting and the location of the game.

It is preferable to get as many parents as possible to attend. Many children want to demonstrate how well they can play in front of Mum and Dad even though they would never tell you so. This desire for reassurance can also be very strong where the parents have separated. Sometimes the parent(s) inform you of the situation, in other cases it only comes out when chatting to the child as to why no parent or only one parent attends the game. Either way, active parental support will invariably improve the player's performance.

## First-Aid Kits

The first-aid kits sold by the large pharmacies are not usually considered suitable for football. Consult your local St John Ambulance

---

> **Tips**
>
> Definitely think twice about refereeing in a Cup game. Bring in a neutral referee, otherwise you are tempting fate, and possibly your life, when emotions run high.

---

representative for what should be carried. Typically the contents would be:

- crepe bandage
- instant ice packs
- triangular bandage
- non-adhesive dressings
- sachets of sterile water for cuts and eyes
- sponge
- gauze swabs
- tissues
- plastic gloves
- non-allergenic plasters

No potions, creams or analgesic sprays of any kind are to be used.

And now that you have all this equipment it is recommended that you attend a first-aid course so that you know how to use it properly!

## MATCH DAY

### Match Day Organization

*Quick Checklist*

- kit
- location map
- balls
- ball pump
- drinks
- first-aid kit
- stud key
- whistle

When you arrive at the opposition's pitch, pace it out to compare its size with your own pitch, as this is important for goalkicks and corners. Pitches on wide open fields can look deceptively large. The size of the pitch may require a change of tactics to protect your wings as well as requiring the backs to move more into the opposition half. You should also check the size of the goals.

You will need to check the wind direction – if the wind is strong then you will probably want to have it on your back in the first half if you win the toss. You should also look for any particularly wet or muddy patches that need avoiding, and whether there is a slope? If there is, then it's usually best to go for downhill in first half if you win the toss. Be aware of the position of the sun – if it is low, is it likely to be in the goalkeeper's eyes?

Next, carry out a warm-up, and check the player's laces. There is nothing worse than seeing a ball flying through the air followed by the boot which has just kicked it. You should also check with the referee as to the policy regarding taking free kicks, ensuring that everybody knows who is the captain and who takes free kicks, penalties, throw-ins and goal kicks.

Some managers indulge in 'ra-ra' sessions whereby they attempt to pump up the players' motivation, and probably their own at the same time. Some of these talks are unintentionally comic, while others fall just short of 'once more unto the breaches'.

You must make sure the toss is taken. Sometimes the opposition will just line up to take advantage of the slope or wind. This is horrendous gamesmanship, so beware. You should also always put out your strongest team first. If you want to experiment you will need a safe comfort zone.

Finally, tell the players to always play to the whistle and to go out, play well, enjoy themselves *and never, never, ever give up.*

## During the Match

During the game, walk around the pitch as it literally provides a view of the game from different angles. Don't necessarily follow the ball – cast your eye about to see where everybody is standing and attempt to assess the overall situation.

---

### Tips

I have absolutely no idea how to motivate young players. Bribery and impassioned appeals have usually failed, so I tend to concentrate on removing what I feel would be the demotivating factors. Ranting, raving, swearing, humiliating and using sarcasm are prime targets for disposal. I wouldn't like to be treated in such a manner, and I suspect nor would you.

In all honesty, if your players are, to the best of your knowledge, at least on a par with the opposition, then if they want to win they will, and if they don't then they won't. It is difficult to believe that some short inspirational flimflam will make up for any inadequacies in training.

---

### Tips

I prefer to keep quiet and provide limited praise and specific instructions as and when required. Just about every other manager seems to prefer a more vocal approach, although I would question whether many of the instructions are heard by the players. The vocal approach usually harmlessly dissipates the manager's frustration, but it can also provide much amusement and entertainment for the spectators.

---

*This short corner looks risky as the defender is racing in to challenge. See how the two Whites are completely unmarked.*

*The ball has now gone loose and even more of the Whites are unmarked and kept onside by the Blue defender coming in off the posts.*

*A free kick has been awarded on the edge of Blue's penalty area. The Blues walk away with their back to the ball and in danger of being caught out by a quickly-taken kick.*

*The obligatory wall is formed, the player is running in to strike the ball, yet five Whites remain unmarked.*

*The free kick hit the underside of the bar and into the net.*

If you do not find it easy to 'read the game', then the following structure may be of assistance for analysing play in a methodical fashion. It commences with the defence and moves forward:

- Are the opponents able to attack easily?

  – Is it an individual or group problem? Would a substitution solve or ease the problem?

- Are the defence able to regain possession when under attack?

  – If it is, is it a case of good defending or poor attacking?

- Does the team make good use of possession?

  – Is the team capable of keeping possession?

- Does the ball move forward in most instances when passing?

  – Is there an active midfield presence? The disappearance of the midfield is a common feature of junior soccer.
  – Is there adequate support for the player with the ball?

- How many shots at goal are made when the player is in a favourable position?

  – Are unnecessary passes being made?
  – Is the ball being held too long? Is it due to lack of support or the player's attitude? If a player is within range of the opposition goal and has just sufficient time and space to take a shot, they should do so. The more shots you take, then all other things being equal, the more goals you will score. Remember – you miss 100 per cent of the shots you never take.

## Tips

As a manager, don't make a fool of yourself by exploding in frustration. For reasons of providing good entertainment, documentaries or films revolving around football always seem to focus on the manager going berserk in the changing rooms at half-time with the players sitting dejected and staring at their boots.
No doubt such behaviour may allow the manager to let off steam, but if the team is doing badly then it is difficult to see how losing your temper will improve matters. While it is doubtful whether such an approach is successful with adults it will certainly destroy youngsters.

- Are there any specific individual problems developing as play progresses?

  - Can these be resolved during the match, or at the next training session?
  - Which side is getting stronger as the game proceeds? Hopefully it will be yours.
  - Consider placing an assistant near the goal to provide support and advise the goalkeeper.

## Half-time

If you are leading 10–0 at half-time nobody is going to learn anything if you score another ten goals in the second half. Suggest to the opposition that you swap over players to give

*This young warrior will rise to fight another day.*

greater balance to the two sides. Huge wins do no favours for either team, although your team may not fully appreciate this point at the time.

At half-time ask the parents to keep clear otherwise each player is taken to one side by a well-meaning parent and told a set of tactics which they feel to be appropriate to their child. The result is that the team now re-assembles with even less of idea of what to do than when it first started. If the first half was good, then simply provide reassurance and praise. If the first half was poor, you must quickly get the players' attention and emphasise the two or three major points for change. However, remember that there is a limit to how much can be absorbed in such a short amount of time.

## Dealing with Errors

If a player has made a bad mistake ensure that they are not left downhearted by providing as much encouragement as you can. Do not criticize them in public; instead, have a quiet word at a more appropriate time. Sometimes if a mistake has been made and a goal conceded, a team will remain in the penalty area and indulge in blaming each other. If you see the opposition do this then you know they are slowly destroying themselves. Under no circumstances must players blame each other during the match. If they concede a goal they must line up quickly for kick-off and commence play again without any kind of recrimination taking place.

---

### Tips

Try to avoid using 'manager logic'. If you lost 3–0 then it is quite pointless saying that the score doesn't reflect the balance of play. Unfortunately it does. If the opposition had three scoring chances and scored three goals and your team had twenty chances and missed the lot, then the score is a perfect reflection of the true state of play. Matches are determined by how many times the ball goes into the net, not how many times it flew over the bar.

Similarly, if you felt your team had the bulk of possession and that they deserved a draw, then the score would have been 3–3. But it wasn't, so while you may have had the majority of possession the sad fact is that you didn't make good use of it.

---

## The End of the Game

- Whether you win or lose, always make sure your team applauds the opposition.
- If you win easily, do not castigate the team for not scoring more goals. If they won then that's good enough.
- It is usual to award a Man or Woman of the Match award at the end of the game. It is an award which needs to be spread around the team, otherwise the major goalscorer is nearly always the winner. Always tell the team what the player achieved during the game which merited the award.

# CHAPTER 13

# So Where Do I Go From Here?

It's the end of the season and you're still in one piece. The team is largely intact, having managed a few wins and have only been hammered once. You've never used the word 'commitment' during the entire season, which in itself is a major achievement. The parents haven't shown signs of mutiny, there has been a definite improvement in the standard of play, you're keen to continue next year, so where do you go from here?

A good starting point would to be go for a holiday, or at the very least forget about football for the next four months. You need a break, the parents are beginning to suffer from football fatigue and the players . . . well, they are probably looking forward to playing cricket.

Another aiming point would be to acquire an FA coaching qualification. Although demanding in terms of time, such a course provides the opportunity to eradicate any drastic flaws in your coaching technique before they become too ingrained. You will gain a lot of confidence and a perhaps a little street credibility in the process. It also provides the opportunity to mix with other managers and realize that that perhaps you are not as bad as you thought and that many of the problems that you've faced are pretty common to most junior football situations. If you get the opportunity to join a course then take it.

There will also be coaching associations within most major cities and towns. You do not have to be a qualified coach to join – just interested in becoming better is quite sufficient. They usually run regular training sessions and these will provide a rich source of ideas for you.

Details of such courses and associations can be obtained from the FA Coaching Information Service, 25 Soho Square, London W1D 4FA. Tel. 0207 4027151.

## Using an External Coach

An alternative course of action could be to use an external, and probably qualified, coach to take some of the training sessions. Certainly bringing in a good outsider is likely to provide an extra boost to training, initially from seeing a new face as the players are probably getting bored with yours, but more importantly from experiencing different ways of coaching.

If this seems a possible way forward, you would be well advised to see the coach in action before making a decision. You have to feel satisfied with their style of coaching and their organizational competency. Also both parties must be quite clear as to what is expected of them and their degree of authority and control. It is unlikely that any partnership will last long if the manager keeps interfering with training sessions.

# Suggested Further Reading

*Soccer Skills, Tactics and Teamwork*
Charles Hughes, FA Director of Coaching and Education
First published 1990 by Diamond Books
ISBN 0752519514

*The FA Coaching Book of Soccer, Skills and Tactics*
Charles Hughes, FA Director of Coaching and Education
First published 1980 by the BBC and Queen Anne Press
ISBN 1 85291 545 5

This provides a very comprehensive guide to all aspects of the game. It has been criticized for its emphasis on direct football and the long ball game, but this aside, there is plenty of good advice to be gleaned from the text.

*The Guinness Book of Skilful Soccer*
Stephen Ford and Colin Wolfinden
First published 1991 by Guinness Publishing
ISBN 0 85112 969 2

*Youth Soccer Coaching*
Tony Carr and Stuart Prosser
First published 1997 by Ward Lock Books
ISBN 0 7 63 7578 5

An excellent book, which while aimed at players aged fourteen and upwards provides ideas and exercises from which younger teams could benefit.

# Index